Christine Schirrmacher

Political Islam – When Faith Turns Out to Be Politics

WEA
World Evangelical Alliance

International Institute for Religious Freedom
IIRF

The WEA Global Issues Series

Editors:

Bischop Efraim Tendero, Philippines,
Secretary General, World Evangelical Alliance

Thomas Schirrmacher,
Director, International Institute for Religious Liberty and
Speaker for Human Rights of the World Evangelical Alliance

Volumes:

"The WEA Global Issues Series is designed to provide thoughtful
and practical insights from an Evangelical Christian perspective into
some of the greatest challenges we face in the world.
I trust you will find this volume enriching and helpful in your Kingdom service."
Bischop Efraim Tendero, Secretary General, World Evangelical Alliance

Christine Schirrmacher

Political Islam

When Faith Turns Out to Be Politics

Translator: Richard McClary
Editor: Thomas K. Johnson
Editor al Assistants: Ruth Baldwin

The WEA Global Issues Series
Volume 16

WIPF & STOCK · Eugene, Oregon

POLITICAL ISLAM
When Faith Turns Out to Be Politics

Copyright © 2016 Verlag fur Kultur und Wissenschaft. All rights reserved. Except for brief quotations in critical publications or reviews, no part of this book may be reproduced in any manner without prior written permission from the publisher. Write: Permissions, Wipf and Stock Publishers, 199 W. 8th Ave., Suite 3, Eugene, OR 97401.

This edition published by Wipf and Stock Publishers in cooperation with Verlag für Kultur und Wissenschaft.

Wipf & Stock
An Imprint of Wipf and Stock Publishers
199 W. 8th Ave., Suite 3
Eugene, OR 97401

www.wipfandstock.com

PAPERBACK ISBN: 978-1-4982-9198-9
HARDCOVER ISBN: 978-1-4982-9199-6

Manufactured in the U.S.A.

Contents

The Compact Series

Does what follows apply to you? As an average citizen, there are numerous topics about which you would like to be informed (or about which you need to be informed). However, what the experts write is normally too complicated and too extensive. Who has the time to take weeks to study every topic at lenth!?

We want to help. In Hänssler's *Compact Series*, experts who have devoted years of intensive involvement to one particular topic give a short and understandable overview of what one should know if he or she wants to be informed and to join the conversation.

For this reason, each volume in Hänssler' *Compact Series* contains the following elements:

- Facts and basic information
- A discussion of controversial questions
- Practical helps and hints for further study

Each volume is arranged so that the reader can become familiar with the basic aspects of a topic within two to three hours (about the time it takes to watch an evening crime story or complete an average train trip). Integrating the knowledge into one's life, or having conversations with others about it will surely take somewhat longer...

I hope that this small volume will broaden your horizon and provide the information you seek.

Thomas Schirrmacher

Publisher's Preface

Islam is obviously one of the greatest challenges facing the church, society, and the political realm today. This challenge arises, for example, in society and politics because Islam exists not only as a religion; it also has numerous rules for coexistence in society. Additionally, it is the opinion of many Muslims –but by no means all! – that Islam also provides the guidelines for an Islamic-based set of public policies and laws. This tack in Islam – political Islam – desires to see a sweeping implementation of Mohammed's standards in all areas of life. Islamists believe that they would finally achieve a leading role in the world if they were able to implement Islam holistically. This means complete compliance with the *sharia*, which is Islamic law applied to marriage and the family. This compliance also requires application in the realm of criminal law, with the sharia's draconian corporal punishment. This was addressed in a prior volume in this series by the same author, *The Sharia*.

At the same time, political Islam or Islamism – in contrast to Jihadism or terrorism – does not necessarily first and foremost have anything to do with violence. On the contrary, the large majority in the Islamic movement turned away from the use of violence long ago and is instead attempting to peacefully exert political and societal influence. Representatives of political Islam are well-trained political strategists who, in suits and ties and via organized Islam and Islamic organizations conduct resolute lobbying activities in Europe in order to promote the implementation of Islamic society.

The author provides a sophisticated overview of the genesis of this global movement, its view of the world, and its goals, and she demonstrates that it is essentially a product of the twentieth century. The reader will additionally gain insight into the Muslim Brotherhood, the first institutionalized form of political Islam. At present it is the most interconnected and successful movement in the world. It is also firmly entrenched in the author's native country, Germany, and in the whole of Europe.

Whoever does not want to cast all Muslims into the same pot but wishes to differentiate among them and whoever, least of all, wants to attribute things to Muslim neighbors which these neighbors do not at all advocate does well to learn just what it is that political Islam promotes in contrast to Islam in general.

Thomas Schirrmacher

Introduction

What is meant by Islamism, or political Islam? Do Islam and political Islam have to be differentiated from each other, or are they congruent with one another? Is not Islam, from its inception onward and on the basis of its principles, actually a political religion, such that making a distinction between Islam and political Islam has to appear artificial? Are there any Muslims at all who separate their religion from politics and practice their faith in a non-political form?

It is an undisputed fact that the founder of Islam, Mohammed, beginning in approximately 610 A.D., emerged with the claim of being sent by God. At the latest when he moved to Medina in 622 A.D., he also became the lawgiver of his first congregation as well as a military leader. The Koran – and more so the written Islamic tradition (Arabic: *hadith*)[1] that accumulated until roughly the tenth century– together contain not only guidelines for the practice of religion or ethics, but also instructions, directed toward Mohammed's followers, about fighting the enemies of the first Islamic community.

During Mohammed's lifetime, defensive warfare and wars of aggression were viewed as legitimate, even as divinely decreed means for implementing Mohammed's leadership claims. Upon Mohammed's death the Koran ended. In order to be able to basically acquit the Koran of any endorsement of war and politics in the name of faith, the Koran is, so to speak, missing anything that corresponds to a New Testament. That is to say, what is missing is content that would depoliticize the directions for political action from the time of Mohammed's life, as in the case with Jesus when he made a call to separate the spiritual from the secular realm. ("So give back to Caesar what is Caesar's, and to God what is God's." Matthew 22:21). One could also look at Paul's admonition to leave the monopoly of force solely to the state (Romans 13:1). This gap for a possible non-political interpretation of the Koran, which Mohammed himself left behind, was not closed by the first centuries of classical Islamic theology, especially since the widespread conquests of Mohammed's successors, the caliphs, continued. Indeed, up until the present day Islamic scholarship at established theolog-

---

[1]   Islamic tradition or *hadith* consists of reports, which, according to majority opinion in Islamic scholarship, were up to the tenth century A.D. recorded in six comprehensive collections considered to be authoritative by Sunnis. Shi'iites accepted different collections of *hadith* referring to the family of Mohammed. From a Muslim point of view, at least the faultlessly reliable narratives of Mohammed, his family, and his companions that have been passed down are binding in all questions of law and are recommended to be emulated in all other areas.

ical institutes and universities has found no recognized approach for reforming the "sword verses" into a generally non-political interpretation.

To be sure, there are those progressive, modernistic, or liberal-thinking Muslim thinkers who are campaigners for freedom and human rights, for enlightenment, and for women's rights, and who are serious proponents of a separation of state and religion. They are speaking decisively against co-opting Islam for political means and are calling for a non-political reevaluation of the source materials. However, their unorthodox views are still pushed to the margins of their societies by the religious and political establishments, so that their positions have little impact on official discourse. Beyond that, numerous mystical movements are principally non-political, as their adherents practice an inwardly turned search for God and submerge into a meditative form of worship. These adherents are also not the ones who would be able to introduce a change in theological direction at universities and mosques.

There are, of course, those who are advocates of a non-political Islam, who are supporters of a separation of the political and religious spheres. They are both theologians and intellectuals, and they speak out for a separation of Islam as a religion from the political message of domination and of jihad in modernity. And there are many more Muslims – or more generally, people from countries and families shaped by Islam – who practice Islam more or less intensively but who conceive of it as a spiritual or ethical message. Besides those mentioned as mystics (Sufis), this could also be traditional or even orthodox believing Muslims who nevertheless advocate the avoidance of a commingling of politics and religion. Whoever maintains there is only "one Islam" anyway – that is, its political wing, Islamism, and its jihadism that is prepared to use violence – and that Muslims who do not confess to holding this stance deliberately mislead their discussion partners, has himself subscribed to the one-sided political view of Islamism that likewise represents the idea that there is only one "true" Islam.

On the other hand, it cannot be overlooked that the twentieth and twenty-first centuries have experienced an unprecedented expansion and powerful demonstration of political Islam, which lays claim to the privilege of interpretation over the Muslim community around the world. All those movements that see Islam as a unity of belief, politics, and social order and that wish to see this all-encompassing system implemented by force or by participation in the exercise of power are part of political Islam. Political Islam does not claim to be one among many possible textual interpretations, but rather to be proclaiming the one acceptable textual interpretation, i.e., of the one, true Islam. That Islamism at its core has to do with politics cum religious justification is what makes it dangerous, since "precisely the

significance and effects of non-violent political activity in Europe and particularly in Germany are wantonly neglected."[2]

In contrast to political Islam, which especially in the last decade has
made public avowals that expressly renounce violence, extremism and
jihadism have explicitly called for the use of force in order to implement
this comprehensive form of Islam and the erection of a caliphate. From
texts in the Koran and from texts belonging to written tradition, jihadism
nowadays finds justification for armed battle, i.e., for "striving in the path
of Allah" – jihad at gunpoint, so to speak.

---

[2]   Frisch, Peter. "Der politische Islamismus," in Foertsch, Volker; Lange, Klaus
(eds.) *Islamistischer Terrorismus. Bestandsaufnahme und Bekämpfungsmöglichkeiten. Berichte und Studien der Hanns Seidel Stiftung*, 86. Akademie für Politik
und Zeitgeschehen: München, 2005, pp. 19-27, here p. 21.

I. What is meant by Islamism or Political Islam?

A. Not necessarily the use of violence ...

Violence was not the central idea of the movement of political Islam at its inception, and the use of violence is not its primary goal. The ideology of political Islam is not explicitly geared toward calls to violence or to a general justification of violence. On the other hand, it does not issue a rejection of the possible use of violence – especially with the justification that it is defense against the enemies of Islam or is in the service of erecting Islamic order in society – seldom turns with word or deed against those who employ violence to implement such goals and often legitimizes violence as a proper means to defend Islam, the Koran or Mohammed.

And there is more: Calling upon the example of Mohammed and emulating him in religious, societal, and political respects, Islamism ideologically prepares the soil for the use of violence, since this comprehensive emulation also includes the Koran-based reports of Mohammed's military campaigns. Since political Islam's concern is a very basic one, one should not prematurely judge a movement to be less alarming just because its paramount concerns are strategic and political and not the exercise of violence.

B. Not necessarily a particularly devout form of Islam ...

The assumption that the concept of political Islam means a theological category within Islam, that is to say, a division of Islam that is marked by conservative or traditional notions, would be misleading. It is not the case – to speak altogether generally – in the region from Tunis to Jakarta, that liberal notions are taught in any explicit sense from the pulpits in mosques and from the lecterns of universities, and that these serve as a basis from which political Islam distinguishes itself by emphatic reference to the eternal validity of the Koran. Nor is it the case that Islamists hold more intensively to Islam as a religion than do other Muslims. Indeed, according to Islamist notions, there is only one single correct interpretation of Islam – and that is the Islamist interpretation. For that reason, Islamists have frequently been designated "fundamentalists." This term is, however, rather indistinct and even basically inapplicable. This is because, as mentioned, political Islam does not have to do with a theological establishment but rather with an ideological justification of Islam as a unified religion, social order, and set of political principles.

Additionally, the leaders of the political Islamic movement have rarely been theologians. In contrast, most of them are theological lay people (frequently members of scientific professions, teachers, journalists, and publicists) and/or autodidacts in the area of theology. Along these lines, Hassan al-Banna, the founder of the first and most significant Islamist movement, the Muslim Brotherhood, was a teacher in a village school and had no particular theological training. Regardless, Islamists, just as jihadists, claim to have the privilege of interpretation when it comes to Islam in that they define what the "one true Islam" is and wherein unbelief exists.

On the other hand, conservative or traditionally thinking Muslims in do not automatically tend toward or more easily tend toward political Islam or radical ideas. An intensive religious practice or traditional piety is not an automatic precursor for politically motivated notions about Islam or the exercise of violence. There are additional factors that have to be added to the mix. Therefore, it is not helpful to allege that Muslims who simply live according to the ethical rules of Islam are adherents of political Islam or even extremists. If it were actually true that adherence to Islam automatically led to the use of violence, there would not only be al-Qaeda terrorists, IS warriors and other similar movements. There would also be hundreds, if not thousands, of additional such groups, and our world would lie in ruins.

C. ... but a political ideology

When it comes to the topic of Islamism or political Islam, one is dealing with nothing less than a conflict with a totalitarian ideology. It is a totalitarian ideology that uses religious terminology while demanding to put the original form of the Islamic faith comprehensively into practice. Political Islam is an ideology – and not a realistic roadmap for coping with the present – because it does not convey a practical concept of the actions to be taken to realize its utopian picture of the world. Rather, it always assumes a current state of affairs that is disadvantageous and has to be overcome as well as a future condition that is desirable and in which all people can expect peace and justice. In the process, the question of how, in actual fact, the introduction of a comprehensive form of Islam could address or solve existing negative societal and political developments remains completely unanswered. These negative developments include the inadequate infrastructure of many regions where Islam is the shaping force, rural flight, the educational plight, the high level of unemployment and lack of prospects, and the high level of illiteracy.

Political Islam pursues a political agenda which cannot be reconciled with the basic principles of democracy, due process, and individual civil rights and liberties. Since political movements within Islam mostly speak about themselves less dramatically than as being extremism that is prepared to use violence and is responsible for numerous attacks, the potential danger of political Islam is less directly recognizable as a danger to the state and democracy, especially as its ideological substructure and claim to power are less clearly labeled or not truly taken seriously. Political Islam is nevertheless a model for explaining the world with explosive force in the heads and hearts of people, because it commits them to an alleged desirable life in the utopia of an archetypal Islamic society. At the same time, it leads them to reject their fellowman and their own lives in the present society as substandard and calls them into action in creating a totalitarian world order. The point is that in the process, political Islam – when it comes to western society – exploits democratic mechanisms and freedoms for its own cause in order to conduct what we might call a "march through the institutions" more than to present a direct declaration of war with the aid of armed force.

For this reason alone, it is essential to acquaint oneself with the basic concerns, causes, and personalities within political Islam around the world and in western societies. On the one hand, it would be unwarranted to place all Muslims under the general suspicion of being politically dangerous, which would help contribute to driving apolitical democratic citizens into the arms of the hardliners of political Islam. On the other hand, it has to be clearly recognized where political personalities are advancing their political agenda for their own purposes.

D. Islamists' agenda in ten points

Political Islam is synonymous with a socio-political ideology supported by a religious justification, the goal of which is to perfectly implement the Koran and the *sharia* and thus to reestablish the archetypal Islamic society.

1.   Unity within the Muslim community (Arabic: *umma*)

Islamists proclaim that there is only one community of all Muslims and that all forms of separation among the divergent legal schools and denominations are wrong. The unity of the entire Muslim community means that national borders are unimportant. This is all the more the case since the emergence of modern nation states in the Middle East at the time of colonialization is closely tied to the western influence of people they regards as "Zionists and crusaders." Islamists also look at the existence of the numerous Sunni and Shiite legal schools within Islam as wrong, since there should only be one form of Islam. Based on the fact of the unity of God (Arabic: *tauhid*), which is the basis of all Islamic theology, the goal of Islamists is to produce this unity in the world through the generation of a unified Islamic community with a belief and a leader, a caliph, as the mirror image of the uniqueness and unity of God.

What becomes clear in this ideal of unity is the ideological and unrealistic character of political Islam. It can hardly be expected that the doctrinal differences of the many different groups and the mutual rejection of each other by Sunnis and Shiites, growing for centuries, could somehow quickly disappear into thin air as the Islamists hope. Since the prevailing majority of Islamists is influenced by Sunnite Islam, they of course expect acceptance of Sunnite teaching by the Shiite minority. For their part, the Shiite regime of Iran is attempting to export Shiite teaching to the rest of the world by, for instance, means of Islamic revolution.

2. The sole eternal validity of the Koran and the exemplary habits Mohammed exhibited (Arabic: *sunna*)

All the questions posed by modernity relating to the areas of belief, society, and politics should be assessed and treated on the basis of the guidelines set out by the Koran and tradition (Arabic: *sunna*: obligatory imitation of the habits of Mohammed). In so doing the exclusivity and universal validity of the Koran and the *sunna* are, on the one hand, emphasized. On the other hand, there is a call for a basic reevaluation of all questions not addressed in the Koran and the *sunna*. This reevaluation should occur with a view to strictly following all the principles laid down in the Koran and in tradition. With this, Islamists call for the "opening of the gate of independent reasoning" (Arabic: *ijthihad*: discrete reevaluation of a question in accordance with timeless valid principles), that is, a revitalization of Islamic jurisprudence. This revitalization means a repression of all non-Islamic elements (e.g., from colonial times), as well as a rejection of every secularly based law.

3. The comprehensive use of the *sharia*

The goal of Islamist groups is the comprehensive implementation of the *sharia* under the leadership of a caliph, that is, in the final outcome, the erection of a theocracy. Neither elected representatives of the public in a secularly oriented democracy nor a dictatorship is viewed by Islamists as a legitimate form of governing. The goal of political Islam efforts is the erection of a caliphate throughout the entire Muslim community, since the caliphate, as an early Islamic and thereby sole exemplary form of rule, is considered valid. It is also seen as exemplary because the caliphate represented the unity of worldly and spiritual rule during the times of the first four successors of Mohammed, the four "rightly guided caliphs" (Arabic: *al-khulafa' ar-rashidun*). These 29 years of caliph rule, from the time of Mohammed's death in 632 A.D. until 661 A.D., are designated as the "golden age of Islam." Political movements of Islam aspire to achieve a restoration of early Islamic superiority and expansive force. In such a caliph-led state, the *sharia* has to be comprehensively employed in law relating to marriage, family, and inheritances, as well as in law relating to commerce, crime, foundations, and trusts.

4. A comprehensive approach to Islam

Islamists only accept a form of Islam that imitates Mohammed as comprehensively as possible. In its justification, political Islam essentially refers to the so-called "Medinan" Islam, i.e., the last ten years of Mohammed's life (622 A.D. until 632 A.D.), which he spent in Medina as a military leader and a lawgiver after moving from his native city of Mecca. For this reason, Islamists deny that there is any difference at all between Islam and political Islam. According to their view of things, there is only "the (comprehensive) Islam," and they refuse to accept the term Islamists for themselves. If politics and religion are defined as an inseparable unity, then, of course, a differentiation of the two spheres has to appear to be artificial and incorrect, and Islam's claim as a legal and societal order can be reduced under no circumstances.

5. Islam as an answer to all questions

The slogan of the Islamist-oriented Muslim Brotherhood reads: "Islam is the solution!" (Arabic: *al-Islam huwa l-hall*). Islam is comprehensive and sufficient to answer all the questions and meet all the demands in all the areas of human life. Islam defines the task, principles, and way of life in life here and now, and it possesses all of the answers to the questions mankind has anywhere in the world. These answers are not to be found outside of Islam, and the problems within human society are not to be solved without implementing Islamic principles. At the same time, Islamists' use of the word "solution" in the slogan is indistinct enough to be able to agree with various movements that have assorted different strategies within the overall Islamist movement.

6. The use and simultaneous rejection of modernity

Political Islam is neither anti-modern nor medieval. It intensively utilizes the achievements of modernity (in particular, communication over the internet and satellites but also through the use of modern medicine, banking, and the areas of explosives and weapons technology). However, political Islam does not view these as indications of progress but rather as tools for the advancement of their message. They take them into their service, and it is from this perspective that Islamists have their eye on modernity. Islamists, on the other hand, are at the same time anti-modern, since all humanizations of Islamic criminal law and all adjustments to modernity, enlightenment, or pluralism are rejected by Islam. The goal is not a Europeanization of Islam in the sense of a "Euro-Islam" but rather an Islamification of modernity or Europe, as the case may be. Islam and its timelessly valid revelation, as it is stipulated in the Koran, in tradition, and in the *sharia*, maintain the character of law. This timelessly valid revelation does not have to be reformed, adapted to modernity, or toned down in its demands; rather, modernity must cater to Islam.

7. Progress through regress

Political Islam copes with the present and the future by its orientation toward the past. By declaring the "golden age of Islam," i.e., the period of Mohammed's rule and that of the first four caliphs up to the year 661 A.D., to be the ideal legal and societal order, political Islam declares a return to the societal order of the seventh century A.D. to be progress, indeed, to be a restoration of a way of life that had been lost but that was just and authentically determined by divine principles. From this perspective, modern constitutions and laws relating to freedom and equality, as well as to democracy and the separation of religion and the state, are condemned as reprehensible. That even in most countries shaped by Islam the comprehensive practice of the *sharia* has been abandoned is, according to Islamist opinion, the reason for the present decline. If, however, a return to the original form of Islam were to be initiated, as it is revealed in the reports of Islamic tradition, a strengthening of Islam would occur, and its leadership role within national groups and religious communities would be able to be asserted.

8. Political Islam as a protest movement

In contrast to the assumption that political Islam is first and foremost a declaration of war against the western world or even against Christianity, it is above all the expression of an intra-Islamic social and political crisis as well as a sign of the dispute over the question of what "true Islam" is. Is it primarily a personal or primarily a publicly expressed faith? Is it ethics and a way of life? A model of how society should look? A political order? Or does Islam encompass all of the areas of life mentioned? That this question has been answered so differently over the course of Islamic intellectual history hangs together with the absence of an ultimate teaching authority in Islam and with the lack of a comprehensive confession of faith and conciliar documents, even if they were only for individual theological "denominations" such as the Shiites or the Sunnis.

In the first instance, political Islam directs itself toward its own society as one shaped by Islam, which, from the point of view of political Islam, is non-Islamic or, in the best case, only externally Islamic. Governments of Muslim majority countries are accused of tyranny, corruption, underdevelopment, powerlessness, dependence upon western countries, and, above all, an inadequate implementation of Islam. They are seen as theologically and societally misguided, and from the time of the mastermind of political Islam, Sayyid Qutb, in the middle of the twentieth century, they have also been viewed as non-believing by many islamists.

For that reason, political Islam, with its comprehensive and political understanding, stands in almost uniform opposition to its own governments, which, as rulers, see themselves as legitimized through their descent from Mohammed's family and from the implementation of the *sharia*. However, they are for the most part criticized by Islamists for pursuing a too western and too little Islamic course and for not uncompromisingly putting the *sharia* into practice. Only as a second step do Islamists view the western world as a geographic area in which the *sharia* should be erected.

9.   The proximity to other totalitarian world views

Political Islam is intellectually closely related to movements such as Salafism and Wahhabism. Salafism is an interpretation of Islam that raises the "pure" Islam that was allegedly practiced in a quintessential manner by ancestors (Arabic: *as-salaf as-salih* and, for that reason, Salafism) up to the position of the measure of all things, which copes with modernity by calling for a cleansing of present-day Islam of all non-Islamic aspects and which alone accepts the Koran and the exemplary customs of Mohammed (Arabic: *sunna*) as correct belief. According to the views of Wahhabi Muslims, cleansing Islam occurs through, for example, forbidding folk Islamic practices as they are expressed in various activities. An example in countries shaped by Islam is the almost universal practice of visiting holy shrines. It also prohibits every other type of "superstition."

The main focus of Salafism lies in the personal way of life, which should be brought into line with the time and practice of Mohammed as much as possible and as far as this can be drawn from tradition. Among the forefathers are Mohammed's direct contemporaries, the "companions of the Prophet," their successors, and, in turn, the following generation, i.e., three generations after Mohammed. Salafists place the focus of their preaching on the call to turn from sin and from all evil, i.e., to turn from everything that is non-Islamic, especially everything that is western and liberal. Salafists in part advocate the use of force in order to bring about this type of return of Islam to its original form.

In addition, political Islam demonstrates a proximity to Wahhabism. Wahhabism, as far as ideology is concerned, is not distant from Salafism. It goes back to Muhammad ibn 'Abd al-Wahhab (1703/4-1791/2), who, beginning in 1744, was able to achieve a lasting political enforcement of his puritanical interpretation of Islam through his links to 'Abd al-Aziz, the head of the al-Sa'ud Beduin tribe. The Puritanism of Wahhabism, so-called after al-Wahhab, called for a return to the Koran and *sunna* to the exclusion of all else, the implementation of the *sharia*, and a permanent "striving in the path of Allah" i.e., *jihad*. al-Wahhab rejected the practice of visiting graves and the veneration of saints, as well as tobacco, alcohol, music, and Islamic mysticism. al-Wahhab especially emphasized the absolute unity of God (Arabic: *tauhid*), which strictly forbade placing anything next to God, i.e., practicing polytheism (Arabic: *shirk*), which would inevitably mean a relapse into paganism (Arabic: *jahiliyya*). According to al-Wahhab's view, this polytheism could, for instance, be expressed by revering a king (in place of God) or by praying to a prophet, a shrine, or some object. Due to the growing influence of Wahhabism in the nineteenth and twentieth centuries, several places of pilgrimage in Najaf and Kerbela, as well as numerous graves of members of Mohammed's family, were destroyed in order to prevent there being a basis for "idolatry" by visiting those locations. Mohammed's grave in Medina has, in fact, been maintained, but those of numerous companions of the Prophet have not. Wahhabites view the second largest Islamic denomination, Shi'ism, to be a sectarian movement.

One major difference between Wahhibism and Salafism lies in the question of rightful governance: While Wahhabites acknowledge tribal heads of Saudi tribes as rulers as long as they aid in the implementation of the *sharia*, Salafites seek a restoration of a caliphate over the entire Islamic community. Today, however, Salafites acknowledge, in part, the installation of a local emir as an interim solution until the establishment of a global caliphate.[3]

10. Political Islam as an ideology of domination

Political Islam not only claims to have the sole appropriate theological interpretation of the message of Islam and its implementation in society but also maintains its direct effectiveness with respect to a desired reallocation of the established balance of power. If more people – first of all Muslims – would comprehensively put Islam in its pure form into practice by follow-

---

[3] "Wahhabism," in Roy, Oliver, Sfeir, Antoine (eds.) *The Columbia World Dictionary of Islamism.* Columbia University Press: New York, 2007, pp. 398-404, here p. 399.

ing early Islamic teaching and practice, there would be a recovery of the power, reputation, and dignity of the early Islamic age that existed when spiritual and worldly rule lay in a single hand. Islamists' wishes are thus not theoretical theological considerations or social reforms alone. What is at issue is laying claim to a pioneering and leadership role in the world over against all other, especially non-Muslim, countries.

This claim is made clear in the desire and ambition of organizations of political Islam in western societies to be a (preferably the only) point of contact for the church, society, and politics and to be able to speak for the entire Islamic community. Moreover, organizations of political Islam also desire to capture the entire community of Muslims for their own goals by exercising intense influence on mosques and other networks. In this connection, the efforts of many an Islamist- oriented organization or association to be dominant when it comes to public communiqués regarding Islam and Muslims are particularly observable. They claim this position by using the democratic right to have a say in matters while not approving the contents of democracy in politics and in matters of security policy. They place spearheads for a political Islam in influential positions with the aid of scholarships and logistical support, or they call for recognition of minority rights with the aid of propaganda trials that gain media attention, in order to emphatically, and with effective public publicity, lay claim to the role of a type of political avant-gardism in Europe.

E. A 10-point summary of Islamists' model for understanding the world

1. Islam is a comprehensive system for the individual, society, and politics. It is wrong to reduce one's understanding of Islam to the area of personal faith, and such action is responsible for decline in countries shaped by Islam.

2. The Koran and the exemplary customs of Mohammed (Arabic: sunna) comprise the sole foundation and standards for a configuration of everyday life that pleases God. It is from this position from the seventh century that modernity is evaluated and fashioned.

3. The blind imitation of the Islam (Arabic: taqlid) practiced by forefathers is objectionable, since, in such cases, it is only employable for questions that are addressed in tradition. Islam has to be applied to present-day circumstances and not adjusted or watered down in its requirements.

4. The sharia is the eternally valid, perfectly divine law that, independent of all western influence, has to be put into practice. No cuts may be made in either theory or practice with respect to the sharia.

5. The reasons for the downfall experienced by countries shaped by Islam and their having dropped behind in the areas of science, the military, commerce, education, and infrastructure lie in departing from "true Islam."

6. By returning to "true Islam" these countries would regain their identity, which has been lost through their dependency upon the West. Additionally, this would bring about pride, honor, well-being, and power in this world, as well as a reputable standing before God in the life hereafter.

7. All of the achievements of modernity have to be justified by Islam and brought into the service of Islam in order to counter the danger of secularization or of blocking out areas that are not saturated with Islam.

8. The goal and conclusion of this reorientation of societies shaped by Islam all the way to implementing Islam is the erection of a just, humane, God-fearing, peaceful society.

9. The means to this comprehensive implementation of Islam is "striving in the path of God" (Arabic: jihad). According to the view of all leading thinkers within political Islam, this is something that has to be carried out. However, for Islamists the militant variation of jihad is not the only interpretation of the term. Preaching and proclaiming true Islam, as well as financially supporting jihad fighters or litigators, also count.

10. The militant wing of political Islam, jihadism, pursues the notion that militant jihad is the unconditional duty of each individual and that this will directly repel evil and bring about the successful Islamification of society and of the entire world. According to the jihadist view, the downfall countries shaped by Islam have experienced is also held to be seen in the misguided assumption that jihad only means to peacefully "go along God's way."

F. Expectations of the future by adherents of political Islam

According to the Islamists' point of view, a consequence of this comprehensive observance of Islam will be an Islamic heyday, a renewed superiority over western culture and society, with progress and well-being, honor and high standing. A just, peaceful society would emerge and all forms of oppression and injustice would come to a halt. Solutions would be found for present-day social problems.

At this point the ideological and unrealistic nature of political Islam is particularly clear. With only a few exceptions, movements of political Islam have failed to give an answer regarding how numerous social problems and crises in countries shaped by Islam can be remedied through a thoroughgoing implementation of Islam. For example, how would having women completely veiled, which Islamists maintain is prescribed, lead to positive changes practically occurring on their own with respect to education problems and the comparatively high rate of illiteracy in numerous countries shaped by Islam? To what degree would individual countries be able to improve their weak infrastructure, their housing shortage in large cities, or the situation of flight from rural areas by fully implementing the *sharia*, i.e., particularly, Islamic marital and criminal law? Will illiteracy and underdevelopment be combated by flogging consumers of alcohol and adulterers? And will more affluence be achieved by only carrying out divorce according to Islamic marital law? Hardly likely! If one excludes Iran and the Islamic Revolution that was proclaimed in 1979, there would be no example of an opposition-led movement of political Islam where evidence could be brought forth that in the case of a change of power, the actual problems at hand could be effectively resolved.[4] Egypt's short-lived experience with a government of the Muslim Brotherhood from 2012 to 2013 is only a proof for this assumption.

Although movements of political Islam have propagated their convictions for approximately 100 years and have exercised societal as well as political influence, up to the emergence of the "IS" (the so-called "Islamic State") neither a caliphate nor a leadership elite founded upon Islam has

---

[4]   One of the leading Islamic representatives, the legal expert, book author and preacher Yusuf al-Qaradawi, defends himself against this charge, in which he maintains that political Islam (Islamism) is very much in the position to offer concrete programs in order to solve known problems but that it does not have to do this since at the present, first of all the "radical re-orientation of society" has to be advanced. Wenzel-Teuber, Wendelin. *Islamische Ethik und moderne Gesellschaft im Islamismus von Yusuf al-Qaradawi. Nur al-hikma. Interdiszplinäre Schriftenreihe zur Islamwissenschaft, Bd. 2.* Verlag Dr. Kovac: Hamburg, 2005, p. 279.

been able to be installed. Part of the attraction of "IS" is the idea of establishing a new global community of all Muslims without national borders and denominational differences. But at the same time, the fragmentation between Sunnis and Shiites has become more competitive, and their bitter hostility toward each other appears to be more insurmountable than ever before.

The social crisis has heightened in many parts of those countries highly influenced by Islam, as has the military and financial dependency upon grants and funds provided for development by western countries. The corruption and despotic nature of many rulers of Muslim majority countries some of who legitimate their positions by military power or by calling upon their ancestral ties to Mohammed's family or, in other cases, claim to have established an "Islamic" regime is ever-present. Indeed, these Islamic leaders are so threatened by the propaganda and willingness on the part of jihadist groups to use violence within their own countries that they have had to seek refuge with western financial backers, secret intelligence services, and military supporters. It is obvious today that in several Islamic regions marked by crisis, there are hardly any independent solutions. Furthermore, without western advice and military and developmental aid, there seems to be hardly any way out of the downward spiral. On the other hand Western politics in some cases definitely contributed to the ongoing crises.

II. The origins of political Islam

For a comprehensive understanding of the history of the impact of political Islam, what follows is an outline of the history of its emergence as well as its spiritual roots and its masterminds. Political Islam is a phenomenon of modernity and derives its justification from within the history of Islam, indeed from early Islamic times. It raises the question of why the most important movements of political Islam all developed either near the beginning of or during the twentieth century and why, practically without exception, the leading personages of political Islam at the present time lean ideologically upon the leading personalities of political Islam dating from the twentieth century.

A. Masterminds of the movement

As early as the end of the eighteenth century and the beginning of the nineteenth century, there were various reform movements and reformed theologians embracing the idea of reform who belong to the list of spiritual precursors of political Islam.

First of all, there was the political activist and philosopher Jamal ad-Din al-Afghani (1839-1897) and after that the legal scholar Muhammad Abduh (1849-1905) and his student, Rashid Rida (1865-1935). As early as al-Afghani, there arose the idea of the necessity of basic reform and restoration of the unity of the Islamic community, the adoption of scientific innovations, and the simultaneous rejection of political and economic influence from Europe in order to help the Islamic world to new strengths and leadership.

The most important student al-Afghani had was the legal scholar, mufti (scholar of theology who issues legal opinions), and journalist Muhammad Abduh, together with his student and successor Rashid Rida, who surely was the most important reform theologian at the turn of the twentieth century. In light of the backwardness of countries shaped by Islam, the causes of which Abduh believed to be an incomplete implementation of Islam, he preached the necessity of setting out on the path toward modernity. Mohammed Abduh, a graduate of the most significant Sunnite university, al-Azhar in Cairo, primarily concerned himself with the possible causes in his writings and sermons. In connection with combating backwardness in the Near and Middle East, he also acknowledged the necessity of far-reaching reform.

Abduh showed a fundamental openness to grappling with non-Islamic world views and, like al-Afghani, he advocated the adoption of scientific as well as technical achievements from Europe. At the same time, he warned against simultaneously assimilating European religious views, philosophies, or values. According to Abduh, Muslims could adopt technical achievements from the West without a need to carry over the worldview framework found in western countries. Since Islam is the religion of reason and the intellect which provides a sufficient worldview, the integration of European scientific achievements should not lead to a contradiction with Islamic values. For that reason, he pleaded for education and instruction in order to teach people what actual Islam is. At this point, one clearly sees the basic orientation toward seeing Islam as the answer to crises in one's own community.

On the one hand, Abduh indeed preached, in Salafitic manner, the cleansing of Islam from everything that was non-Islamic. However, he recognized the solution of the present crisis not in a return to the past but rather in taking steps into modernity (a modernity steeped in Islamic principles) "seeking ... a more rational understanding and presentation of Islamic truth."[5]

Abduh's most important student and successor, the Koran commentator Rashid Rida, developed the thought of al-Afghani and Abduh. Rida recognized that holding fast to "blind traditionalism" was a reason for the demise of Islam. For that reason he advocated, as did Abduh, a cleansing of Islam from everything that is non-Islamic and a return to the original Islam of Medina. According to Rida, this was only possible if – and at this point he goes a step further than al-Afghani and Abduh – there is a restoration of the caliphate and an institutionalized assembly of counselors made up of Muslim theologians (Arabis: *shura*) at the side of the caliph. With this, Rida developed, out of early Islam, a concrete model for rule in the present era. He pursued this thinking in a practical manner with the founding of a training school for the education of his new elite and to attempt to revive the idea of the caliphate.

The comprehensive implementation of the *sharia* was for Rida an essential instrument for coping with the current crisis within Islam. The crisis was for him a result of the attitude of compromise that had been held in this connection. For that reason, Rida found every form of secularization or separation of religion and politics to be objectionable. He made it unmistakably clear that the *sharia*, including its penal code, was an indispensable component of this new and aspired-to order: "...those Muslim [rulers] who introduce novel laws today and forsake the Shari'a enjoined upon them by God. ... They thus abolish supposedly ‚distasteful' penalties such as cut-

---

5   Watt, W. Montgomery. *Islamic Fundamentalism and Modernity*. Routledge: London, 1989, p. 53.

ting off the hands of thieves or stoning adulterers and prostitutes. They replace them by man-made laws and penalties. He who does that has undeniably become an infidel."[6] What is meant by Rida's "reformed Islam" is not an Islam that is modernist, enlightened, or otherwise divested of its political consequences. To be sure, it is oriented toward modernity, but at the same time, with its comprehensive implementation of the *sharia*, it is exclusively directed toward a restoration of the early times of Islam.

When the movement of political Islam of the twentieth century called for a return to the "original" form of Islam, the call was not made with reference only to the reform theologians of the eighteenth and nineteenth centuries but rather with reference to several theologians of early Islamic intellectual history.

These latter include the theologian and legal scholar Ahmad Ibn Hanbal (780-855 A.D.), who was the founder of the strict Hanbalite legal school. An important point of reference for modern political Islam is, in addition to Ahmad Ibn Hanbal, the theologian Ibn Taymiyya (1263-1328 A.D.). Ibn Taymiyya is not only considered an important reference figure for political Islam but also for jihadism, he being perhaps the most significant historical proponent of today's concept of jihad.

Ibn Taymiyya's biography was marked by the invasion and victory of the Mongolian armies over the Abbasides in 1258 A.D. Ibn Taymiyya's own family had to flee out of the north, which today is part of Turkey, to Damascus, while Syria fell to the Mamlukes. Also the armies of the crusades had not yet been driven out of the Middle East. Ibn Taymiyya himself lived as a refugee among what initially were non-Muslim ("pagan") Mongolians (the Ilkhanes), who later converted to Islam. He still viewed them as non-believers. In a very literal interpretation of the Koran and tradition – since he viewed both of these as the true and, for that reason, sole reliable sources – he developed a teaching of jihad in which combat against unbelievers became the unconditional duty of each believer. Islam, according to Ibn Taymiyya, had to be purified from all that was non-Islamic, such as the veneration of saints, which was superstition, i.e., all "innovations" which had to be repudiated. As early as Ibn Taymiyya, the idea arose that misled leaders who did not apply the *sharia* were lapsed Muslims who were still locked in pre-Islamic ignorance (Arabic: *jahiliyya*).[7] This abstract concept later became formative in the thinking of Sayyid Qutb, who

---

[6]   Emmanuel Sivan. *Radical Islam: Medieval Theology and Modern Politics*: New Haven: Yale University Press, 1990, p. 101.

[7]   According to the article "Ibn Taymiyya" in Roy, Olivier; Sfeir, Antoine (eds.) *The Columbia World Dictionary of Islamism*. Columbia University Press: New York, 2007, pp. 136-137, here p. 136.

was the driving force, or *spiritus rector*, of the Muslim Brotherhood movement.

Ibn Taymiyya's jihadist orientation influenced the Wahhabites, Islamists such as Sayyid Qutb, the Indian proponents of an Islamic state based upon the *sharia* such as Abu l-A'la Maududi, jihadists groups like the "Islamic jihad" under Muhammad al-Faraj in Egypt, and jihadist leaders such as Osama bin Laden. Ibn Taymiyya is considered by jihadist movements to be groundbreaking because he lived in a time of crisis which jihadists view as comparable to modernity in numerous ways. For that reason, his opinions also lead the way in judging and finding solutions in modernity.[8]

However, there were not only internal factors relating to a return to the original form of Islam that were impulses in connection with the development of Islamists' construct of ideas. There were external factors as well.

At the threshold of modernity, the Islamic world found itself well into a lengthy process of decline; this was primarily seen in contrast to western countries: The Ottoman Empire – the last caliphate – had been experiencing a process of geographic reduction and internal decay. The countries of the Middle East had very clearly fallen behind Europe in technology, military affairs, education, and science, among other spheres of life, as a result of the very late permission granted by conservative theologians, beginning in 1784, to operate printing presses. In addition to that, primarily British and French colonial rule in regions marked by Islam from northern Africa all the way to Iraq had left behind deep political and economic incisions. For example, the educational system, with its traditional religious form of instruction, faced competition from a European-language, elite form of education. The Turkish Republic was founded in 1923/1924 and the caliphate was abolished; *sharia* courts were closed; and in 1926 a comprehensive legal codification took place which resulted in religious institutions losing more and more of their influence.

B. The collapse of reformed Islam

Various approaches for political renewal movements came about as answers to what was believed to be the threat of modernity. Reformed Islam of the nineteenth century was not to achieve any lasting success, although it at first had the desire to tie in to Islam's historical position of superiority. Initially, a distinct openness toward the outside had been recognizable,

---

8   According to Riexinger, Martin. "Missbrauch der Religion? Die religiösen Hintergründe des Islamismus (und ihre Verdrängung)" in Möller, Reinhard (ed.) *Islamismus und Terroristische Gewalt. Bibliotheca Academica, Reihe Orientalistik, Band 8*. Ergon: Würzburg, 2004, pp. 29-54, here p. 51.

which then, however, turned into a restriction whereby Islam was defined as the sole source of all knowledge and science.

Muhammad Abduh's concept of a purely external adoption of European scientific discoveries and knowledge, without accepting or even discussing the roots of this knowledge in Europe's worldview and intellectual history, led to a certain interest in the natural sciences, technology, and military affairs. But Abduh's concept did not lead to an open theological discourse with the goal of reconciling conservative Islamic theology with changed relationships toward modernity among countries shaped by Islam. There was no acceptance of pluralization and democratization or pushing back of religion when it came to the mosques and education. On the contrary, re-formed Islam developed into a political and, at the same time, a utopian instrument for a return to the past. So it was that Islamic reformed theology collapsed. It failed in its demand to reinstate the caliphate and to produce a new community of all Muslims (Arabic: *umma*) without national bounda-ries as well as a just and affluent society. It also failed in its aspirations for an economic and scientific upswing and a strengthening of Islam through a return to its roots and the practices of early Islam.

The economic decline continued throughout the nineteenth and twentieth centuries, while dependency upon Europe grew. The influence of European colonial rule was present in the Middle East, as was the progressively un-folding social crisis, which demonstrated itself in a more intense manner through increasing flight from rural areas, poverty, a far-reaching educa-tional plight, missing infrastructure, and, broadly speaking, underdevelop-ment in general. The ruling elite in the individual countries was perceived to be corrupt; personal liberties continued to be sharply curbed; and a his-torical-critical religious and societal discourse in the public realm was only carried out in a very limited manner or was not possible at all.

There were several further milestone events which led to a feeling of disenfranchisement: the final abolishment of the caliphate in 1923/1924; the futile attempt, primarily by Rashid Rida, to reactivate the caliphate in years following; the Balfour Declaration in 1917 which led to the creation of a "Jewish homeland" in Palestine; and finally the founding of the state of Israel in 1948. They heightened existing tensions, as did the traumatic Arab defeat at the hands of Israel in the Six-Day War in 1967, nearly 20 years later. Alliances on the basis of the Arab brotherhood and Islamic identity, such as the short-lived federation entitled the United Arab Repub-lic from 1958-1961, including Syria-Egypt, were as little able to resist long-term strains as were the ideological transfer and the orientation to-ward the Soviet Union as a socialist sister state and lasting partner. All of the concepts relating to the theology of reform, nationalism, pan-Arabism, socialism, liberalism, and the idea of the caliphate collapsed in respect of an overall development of the region. For this reason, in the course of the twentieth century, the return to one's own roots, history, and identity – "true Islam" – seemingly appeared to provide the only acceptable basis for an entry into the modern age: The ideologizing and politicization of the reform movement had begun.

C. The formation of the Muslim Brotherhood in 1928

What came into effect as modern political Islam is very closely tied to the emergence of its first institutionalized organization, the Muslim Brotherhood in Egypt (Arabic: *al-ikhwan al-muslimun*), which is today's largest and most influential Sunnite movement of political Islam. It was brought into being in 1928, only six years after Egypt's formal independence. The Muslim Brotherhood picked up on the body of thought of reformed Islam from the eighteenth and nineteenth centuries, as well as on the political-ideological legacy of Salafism und Wahhabism, and further developed it. The terminus of consideration was now no longer the theoretical considerations regarding necessary conditions relating to the restoration of the caliphate, but rather the completely practical steps to overcome the inferiority experienced by countries marked by Islam and bring about a restoration of Islamic ethical principles.

> *"God is our objective; The Prophet is our example; the Quran is our law; the jihad is our life; Martyrdom is our goal."*[9]

The founder of the Muslim Brotherhood movement was the village schoolteacher Hassan al-Banna (1906–1949) from Mahmudiyya in the Nile Delta, who through his father, a Hanbalite scholar, enjoyed a traditional education. After training to become a teacher, he held a teaching post in Ismailiyya on the Suez Canal from 1927 to 1946. His father was a graduate of the famous al-Azhar University and an imam (religious leader or, more often, congregational prayer leader). Al-Banna studied the works of Muhammad Abduh and Rashid Rida and was, on the one hand, influenced by strict orthodox puritan works by the Salafists and Hanbalites. However, he also recognized how necessary it was to improve the living conditions of the poor in Egypt. As was the case with most of the founders and leaders of

---

[9]   From the 1935 Muslim Brotherhood program, quoted from the article "Muslim Brotherhood" in: Roy, Olivier; Sfeir, Antoine (ed.) *The Columbia World Dictionary of Islamism*. Columbia University Press: New York, 2007, pp. 235-242, here p. 235.

political Islam and jihadist movements, al-Banna was not a theologian by training.

In 1928 – only four years after the abolition of the caliphate by the Turkish Republic – al-Banna founded the Muslim Brotherhood with six employees of the Suez Canal Company, who, as it were, had the political as well as economic intervention of western governments before their eyes on a daily basis (above all, Great Britain as the colonial ruler). Their initial goal was to provide religious instruction to youth.

> "The members of the Muslim Brotherhood bring a Salafi message (sic), a Sunnite order, a Sufi truth, a political body, a sports association, a scientific and cultural union, a commercial enterprise, and a societal notion."[10]

From the beginning the movement had a twofold objective: the implementation of the *sharia* through the establishment of a government which pursued this goal, as well as the preaching of true Islam, supported by social welfare. From its inception, the concepts of preaching and practical assistance have been extremely successful and have been maintained by the Muslim Brotherhood.

The oath of the Muslim Brotherhood

> "I promise before God, the Highest and Greatest to follow strictly the message of the Muslim Brotherhood, to fight for it, to live according to the rules for its members, to have total confidence in its leader and to obey implicitly at all times, in good times as in bad."[11]

It would be an error, however, to assume that at the beginning the movement was above all socially oriented and only later became politicized. From the beginning, as a follower of Mohammad Abduh and Rashid Rida, al-Banna preached a comprehensive understanding of Islam, which also included armed jihad, the battle to defend Islam, and martyrdom, alt-

---

[10] al-Banna, Hassan. "Risalat al-mu'tamar al-khamis" (open letter to the fifth congress), by the same author "Majmua'a rasa'il al-imam al-shahid Hassan al-Banna" (collected open letters of the martyr Hassan al-Banna). Kairo 1992, pp. 1-22ff., quoted in Lübben, Ivesa. 'Die ägyptische Muslimbruderschaft – Auf dem Weg zur politischen Partei" in Albrecht, Holger; Köhler, Kevin (eds.) *Politischer Islam im Vorderen Orient. Zwischen Sozialbewegung, Opposition und Widerstand. Weltreligionen im Wandel 5.* Nomos: Baden-Baden, 2008, pp. 75-97, here p. 78.

[11] Quoted from the article "Banna, Hassan al-(Egypt)" in Roy, Olivier; Sfeir, Antoine (eds.) *The Columbia World Dictionary of Islamism.* Columbia University Press: New York, 2007, pp. 71-74, here p. 71.

hough al-Banna did not directly call for militant action or for any attacks in Egypt. On the other hand, al-Banna, with his call for a comprehensive Islam and the unconditional role model of Mohammed in all areas of society, never distanced himself from the use of militant means for the purpose of accomplishing his goals.

> *"Islam is the teaching of a faith and the veneration of God, one's homeland and nationality, the state and religion, spirituality and action, the Koran and the sword."*

As early as 1936 the Muslim Brotherhood devised a comprehensive program that called for an end to the party system, the full and complete implementation of the *sharia*, the censure of all cultural events as well as the promotion and observance of Islamic moral concepts, and the prohibition of receiving interest as well as a socially oriented division of wealth. The clear desire for domination and the political implementation of Islam and its principles were bound up with the Muslim Brotherhood's platform, as al-Banna formulated it:

> *"It is within the nature of Islam to rule and not to be ruled, to impose its laws upon all nations and to enforce its power upon the entire planet" (Hassan al-Banna).*

al-Banna was in favor of jihad, which for him, however, did not exclusively have to mean militant "striving in the path of God." The movement grew rapidly. In 1936 the movement was said to have had 800 members, and in 1938 already more than 200,000. In his preaching, which was apologetic or defensive in nature, al-Banna turned his attention against all European cultural influence in countries marked by Islam, which he viewed as corrosive and deleterious:

"Afterwards they [Europeans] were in the position ... of even permeating the political, legal, and cultural systems of the most powerful Islamic countries with their nature. They import their half-naked women into these areas together with their brandies, spirits, and theater, their dance clubs and cheap entertainment, their stories, newspapers, novels, their whims and ludicrous games and vices. They tolerate crime here that they would not put up with in their own countries and adorn this superficial, tawdry world, permeated with the stench of sin and exuding the aroma of vice, for the eyes of misguided, pure-minded Muslims with wealth and prestige and embellish the world of Muslims with class and authority."[12]

Hassan al-Banna: Islam

"Listen, Dear Brother: Our mission is one described most comprehensively by the term 'Islamic', though this word has a meaning broader than the narrow definition understood by most people. We believe that Islam is an all-embracing concept regulating every aspect of life, prescribing for everyone it concerns a solid and rigorous order. It does not stand helpless before life's problems, nor the steps that must be taken to reform mankind.

Some people mistakenly understand that Islam is restricted to religious practices or spiritual exercises. Thus they limit their understanding to these narrow lines. On the contrary, we understand Islam broadly and comprehensively, regulating the affairs of men, in this world and the next.

We do not indulge in this claim nor extend upon it on the basis of our own prejudice; rather it is what we have understood from the Book of Allah and the lives of the early Muslims. If the reader wishes to understand the mission of the Muslim Brotherhood in a sense broader than the mere word 'Islamic', let him take the Qur'an and free himself of any preconceived ideas and judgments. Only then will he understand what the Qur'an is about, and see in it the mission of the Muslim Brotherhood.

Indeed, our mission is 'Islamic' in every sense of the word, so understand by it what you will, but remember your understanding is confined to the Book of Allah, the Sunnah (the exemplary habits) of his Apostle, and the lives of the pious predecessors (may Allah's blessing and peace be upon them). Allah's Book is the foundation and the pillar of Islam, the Sunnah of His Apostle is the explanation and commentary to his Book, while the lives of the Pious Predecessors (Allah's grace be upon them) serve as practical models for those who want to carry out its commands and obey its teachings."[13]

---

[12] Hasan al-Banna, *Between Yesterday and Today*. Quoted by Malise Ruthven, *Der Islam*, Stuttgart 2000, pp. 185ff.

[13] Hassan al-Banna. What is our message? According to http://www.2muslims.com/ directory/Detailed/227082.shtml... (Accessed August 2, 2015).

The Muslim Brotherhood, a quickly growing religious as well as social renewal movement, grew into a mass movement in the years following 1928. In 1948 the Muslim Brotherhood was said to have between 500,000 and 1 million adherents. As early as the 1940s, the Muslim Brotherhood had also a militant wing, the "secret apparatus" or "special order" (Arabic: *nizam al-khass*), a secretively operating political arm. Beginning in 1948, the year Israel was founded, the movement became noticeably more political; additionally it was clearly anti-Semitic in its orientation.

The Muslim Brotherhood was in itself not uniform because its various wings were not united with respect to the question of how the goal of Islamification of the Egyptian society could best be achieved and whether preaching and teaching or political upheaval promised more success. As a result, the Muslim Brotherhood fell repeatedly into conflict with the Egyptian government, which intermittently tolerated the brotherhood and intermittently used it for its own purposes. From time to time the government prohibited and persecuted, arrested, tortured, and executed the Brotherhood's members. After its founding phase in Egypt, the Muslim Brotherhood extended its activities to Europe, primarily to Germany and Switzerland, and established opposition groups in Iraq, Jordan, Libya, Tunisia, and Algeria.

In 1948, because of increased political activity and, in particular, because of the Palestinian conflict and a number of attacks in Egypt, the Muslim Brotherhood was for the first time officially banned by the Egyptian government. As a reaction, members of this "secret organization" shot and killed the Egyptian Prime Minister Nuqrashi Pasha, who had issued the ban. In the following year, 1949, the founder of the movement, Hassan al-Banna, was shot and killed out in the open, presumably by the secret police at the behest of the Egyptian royal house, although al-Banna had personally distanced himself from the assassination of Nuqrashi Pasha and was considered to be a leading figure of the moderate wing of the movement.

The Egyptian government assumed that it had now eliminated the influence of the Muslim Brotherhood, but the opposite was the case. Through his death, al-Banna achieved the status of a martyr. And the movement grew further. One segment of the movement turned from all forms of violence and pushed for a "march through the existing institutions" while another segment became noticeably politicized and radicalized.

For a short time, al-Banna's successor was Salih Ashmawi, who was followed in 1950 by Hassan al-Hudaibi. In the early 1950s the Muslim Brotherhood participated in unrest and supported the so-called "Free Officers" in 1952 in their coup d'état to overthrow the Egyptian monarchy. Jamal 'Abd an-Nasir (Nasser) became president. By 1954, however, the relationship of the Muslim Brotherhood to Nasser had cooled, and they began combating him, since according to them, he had not done enough to institute the *sharia* in Egypt. In 1954 there was an assassination attempt on President Nasser, which was ascribed to the Muslim Brotherhood. Thereafter the Nasser administration took action against the movement with all force. The Muslim Brotherhood was prohibited and its leader arrested. The spiritual leader, Sayyid Qutb, was also arrested. One of the leaders, Abdelqadir Awdah, was executed. From 1954 to 1970 Nasser oppressed the movement with an iron fist, accusing it of collaborating with the British as well as with the CIA.[14] Thousands were thrown into prison. And those who were released had to go underground and remain on the run in order to avoid persecution by the secret police. The Muslim Brotherhood had been declared to be an enemy of the state.

D. The thinker behind the movement: Sayyid Qutb

After Hassan al-Banna's violent death, the Muslim Brotherhood received its ultimate leading figure, Sayyid Qutb (1906-1966), who further deepened and politicized the movement's ideological basis. As its true thinker and author, Qutb gave the Muslim Brotherhood its principal orientation. He was born in 1906 in the Asyut province, and as was the case with al-Banna, Qutb completed studies to become a teacher at the Dar al-ulum training institute in Cairo. Beginning in 1939 he was employed in the educational ministry, and he later became an author, novelist, and journalist. In the years 1948-1950, he completed studies in the USA, where he became an avowed opponent of the west. After his return in 1950, he turned to the Muslim Brotherhood, became a member in 1953, and proceeded to publish the weekly newspaper *The Muslim Brotherhood* (Arabic: *al-ikhwan al-muslimun*).

> *"God is our purpose, the Prophet our leader, the Koran our constitution, Jihad our way and dying for God's cause our supreme objective."*

At the beginning of the 1950s, Qutb preached in favor of the leftist-oriented rule that Nasser exerted, which, however, was not fulfilling the expectations of the movement. When the movement was prohibited in 1954 because of the assassination attempt on President Nasser, Sayyid Qutb was arrested and tortured for the first time. In 1955 he was con-

---

[14]   Beginning in 1956 the CIA is said to have actually financially and militarily supported the Muslim Brotherhood, according to the article "Muslim Brotherhood" in Roy, Olivier; Sfeir, Antoine (eds.) *The Columbia World Dictionary of Islamism.* Columbia University Press: New York, 2007, pp. 235-242, here p. 236.

demned to 25 years of hard labor. Qutb spent ten years of the sentence in prison, where he composed his most important writings and, according to agreed-upon opinion, became essentially radicalized. Both of his most important writings, entitled *Signposts* or *Milestones* (Arabic: *ma'alim fi t-tariq*) and his Koran commentary *In the Shade of the Koran* (Arabic: *fi-zilal al-qur'an*), were composed while he was in prison. They demonstrate the influence of the Indian-Islamic journalist Abu-1 A'la Maududi (1903-1979), who, on the eve of the founding of the state of Pakistan, founded *Jama'at-i Islami*, an organization intended to exert pressure on the implementation of sharia in Pakistan. Maududi spoke out in favor of the duty of conducting permanent jihad and the implementation of God's sovereignty (Arabic: *hakimiyat allah*), which the illegitimate rulers of his time did not implement. Maududi viewed the west as thoroughly decadent, atheistic, and materialistic, and he considered Islamic society to be guilty for its own ongoing decline. Muslims therefore need to return to true Islam and put its principles into practice:

Abu l-A'la Maududi

"But the tragedy is that Islam with which Western civilization happens to be in conflict today is a mere shadow of the real Islam. The Muslims are devoid of Islamic character and morals, ideas and ideology, and have lost the Islamic spirit. The true spirit of Islam is neither in their mosques nor schools, neither in their private lives nor in the public affairs. The Law of Islam does not govern their private or collective conduct."[15]

Sayyid Qutb took up numerous thoughts developed by Maududi in his works and used them with reference to his Egyptian homeland. Qutb saw the pre-Islamic era as a time of ignorance (Arabic: *jahiliyya*), not as a "historical epoch but rather as ... a state of mind,"[16] i.e., a state of unbelief in a Muslim-shaped environment. Qutb's works were forbidden by the Egyptian censorship bureau. He was released for a short time in 1964, only to be taken into custody again a few months later. He was then condemned to death by hanging by the Egyptian government and sent to the gallows in August 1966.

---

[15] S. Abdul A'la Maududi. *The Sick Nations of the Modern Age*. Lahore, 1966, p. 13, quoted by Watt, W. Montgomery. *Islamic Fundamentalism and Modernity*. Routledge: London, 1989, p. 56.

[16] Steinberg, Guido. *Der nahe und der ferne Feind. Die Netzwerke des islamistischen Terrorismus*. C. H. Beck: München, 2005, p. 19.

If one had assumed that with the death of Hassan al-Banna, one of the most important protagonists of the Muslim Brotherhood, the movement would have had the rug pulled out from under it, in the case of Sayyid Qutb, an even greater error was committed. The body of thought and sympathy for the cause of the Muslim Brotherhood could not be dispelled in this way, and neither could an ideology be conquered by torture and imprisonment. Sayyid Qutb's death brought him the status of a martyr, and his writings were more widely read from that time on, in spite of all prohibitions placed upon them. They were passed on and adopted more than at any time during his life.

Sayyid Qutb's writings made him one of the most influential ideologues of the twentieth century. He left political Islam and jihadism an edifice of teaching for justifying jihad and the idea of Islam's sole right to rule. His influence even reached into the Shiite realm, as one sees when Ayatollah Khomeini, the father of the Islamic Revolution in Iran, referred to Sayyid Qutb as the "great Egyptian brother."[17]

Sayyid Qutb concretized what was just a generally held consideration on the part of al-Banna regarding the formation of a truly Islamic society. Qutb did not see preaching and social reform as the only means for returning to true Islam. The required reconfiguration of society, in which man-made laws would no longer be allowed to apply, was to occur in four phases: 1. The withdrawal of truly believing individuals from the surrounding, unclean society; 2. The use of the Avantgarde (Arabic: *tali'a*), a set of elite troops, in order to implement true Islam; 3. The establishment of the rule of God (Arabic: *hakimiyya*) under the *sharia*; and 4. The "excommunication" of those who fail to follow this concept as unbelievers (Arabic: *takfir*).

Jihad

"The Jihad of Islam is to secure complete freedom for every man throughout the world by releasing him from servitude to other human beings so that he may serve his Lord, who is One and who has no associates. This is in itself a sufficient reason for Jihad ...
Anyone who understands this particular character of this religion will also understand the place of Jihad bis-Saif (striving through fighting with the sword), which is to clear the way for striving through preaching in the application of the

---

[17] Quoted from the article "Muslim Brotherhood" in Roy, Olivier; Sfeir, Antoine (eds.) *The Columbia World Dictionary of Islamism.* Columbia University Press: New York, 2007, pp. 235-242, here p. 235.

> *Islamic movement. He will understand that Islam is not a 'defensive movement' in the narrow sense which today is technically called a 'defensive war.'... The reasons for Jihad which have been described in the above verses are these: to establish Allah's authority in the earth; to arrange human affairs according to the true guidance provided by Allah Almighty; to abolish all the Satanic forces and Satanic systems of life and to end the lordship of one man over others since all men are creatures of Allah and no one has the authority to make them his servants or to make arbitrary laws for them. These reasons are sufficient for proclaiming Jihad.*[18] *(Sayyid Qutb)*

A very central concept for Sayyid Qutb – and, at the same time, an intensification of al-Banna's original teaching – is the introduction of his category of ignorance or of paganism (Arabic: *jahiliyya*). While Hassan al-Banna propagated the reformation of Islamic society and its turn toward true Islam to be a type of "directional change," Sayyid Qutb intensified the condemnation of all those who do not follow the comprehensive view of the Muslim Brotherhood for the implementation of the *sharia*. Regardless of their Islamic confession of faith, Qutb openly designated them as unbelievers and the society in which they live as heathen or pre-Islamic. Via an incomplete implementation of Islam and a failure to follow the *sharia*, Islamic society thus becomes a heathen society. In this way Qutb excommunicated all those who did not follow his point of view.

Sayyid Qutb: Paganism

"Dschahilijja ("paganism") means the lordship of men over men or, rather, submission to men instead of God (Allah). It means a rejection of the perfection of God and cajolery towards mortals. In this sense dschahilijja not only constitutes a certain historical period of time, but rather a state of affairs. There used to be such a state of affairs of human conditions. It exists today, and it will perhaps also exist in the future in the shape of dschahilijja, this caricature and mortal enemy of Islam. Always and everywhere people stand before the clear-cut choice: either obey the law of God completely or adopt laws of this or that person. In the latter case one finds himself in the state of dschahilijja. An individual ... has to decide: Islam or dschahilijja."[19]

---

[18] Sayyid Qutb. *Milestones (Ma'alim fi t-tareeq)*. Maktabah Booksellers and Publ.: Birmingham, 2006, pp. 81; 71 (http://www.kalamullah.com/Books/Milestones% 20Special%20Edition.pdf) (15.4.2013)

[19] Quoted from Günter Lerch, *Muhammeds Erben. Die unbekannte Vielfalt des Islam*. Düsseldorf 1999, p. 43.

The *sharia* becomes the sole acceptable measure for law and social order, and the erection of Islamic order (Arabic: *nizam*), as a comprehensive
system becomes the key to addressing modernity. The resistance against
"godless" rulers is made a duty for every believer, whereby Sayyid Qutb
expressly called upon Ibn Taymiyya. For Qutb, a democratic system cannot be reconciled with Islam.

Sayyid Qutb's terminology is also exacerbated with respect to his notion
of *jihad*. Qutb rejects the peaceful variant of the *jihad* concept, which interprets sermons, alms, and Islamic education of one's own children as
forms of *jihad*, as false. Indeed, he does not necessarily define concretely
who has to conduct *jihad* or in what manner *jihad* had to be conducted.
However, Qutb made *jihad* a topic of discussion so generally and with
such sweeping terminology that following generations of jihadists were
able to call upon Qutb, since he basically endorsed the militant variant of
"striving in the path of God" (Arabic: *jihad*).

The goal of the Muslim Brotherhood, at the least since Sayyid Qutb, has
been a political one, namely the establishment of an Islamic state with a
thoroughgoing practice of *sharia* law under the leadership of a caliph and
at the same time the basic rejection of laws made by men, which, for instance, one finds in democracy. The freedom to shape political opinion, to
have parliamentary participation in the formulation of laws, to provide
equal rights for women and minorities, to observe individual civil rights
and liberties, as well as to abolish corporal punishment and the death penalty are in principle not thinkable in an Islamic state although they may be
postponed for strategic reasons. At least so far as influenced by Sayyid
Qutb, the Muslim Brotherhood proves itself to be a proponent of a totalitarian social order.

E. Division within the Muslim Brotherhood

Already prior to Sayyid Qutb's violent death in 1966, there were various
positions and groups within the Muslim Brotherhood. The "classical,"
more moderate Muslim Brotherhood and those groups whose adherents
had in part been former Muslim brothers but now openly advocated violence went separate ways. Because of the narrow ideological and in part
personal interdependence of the Muslim Brotherhood with related movements, the most significant competing groups are shortly introduced below.

1. The Group Following Hassan al-Hudaibi

One must mention the group surrounding the judge Hassan al-Hudaibi
(1891-1973), who was the leader of the Muslim Brotherhood during the

years 1950-1973. Hassan al-Hudaibi belonged to the branch of the Muslim Brotherhood which, after Sayyid Qutb's death in 1966, returned to al-Banna's thoughts about gradually restructuring society by preaching instead of fighting. He repudiated Qutb's later condemnation of Egyptian society as "heathen," as he likewise did with Qutb's thoughts regarding the necessity of erecting God's rule by means of violent upheaval. al-Hudaibi advocated the societal implementation of Islam instead of armed combat, consultation (Arabic: *shura*), and education of the "ignorant," which, unlike Qutb, he did not think was truly heathen.

2. *Jama'at al-Muslimin* – JM (The Muslim Community)

This group, which also called itself "Excommunication and Exodus" (Arabic: *al-takfir wa l-hijra*), was led in the 1970s by the engineer Mustafa Shukri. On the one hand, Shukri preached a complete withdrawal from society and the exemplary establishment of a model primal society as a germ cell for the true Islamic state. With his followers he moved into caves in the vicinity of Assiut and into shared living communities (for this he used the term *hijra*, to indicate the exodus out of a godless society). He conducted marriages among his adherents, in whom Islam was to be lived out in an ideal manner. Renunciation of and isolation from the depraved Egyptian society was practiced by this group. Shukri further radicalized the thinking of Qutb. He believed in an imminent battle with the powers of evil and rejected every type of moderate societal Islamification. In 1977 the *Jama'at al-Muslimin* participated in assassinations of, for example, the former Egyptian minister for Islamic Endowments, Muhammad adh-Dhahabi. In 1978 Shukri was captured and executed, and the group was dashed to pieces.

3. *Jama'at al-Islamiya* - JI (Islamic Community)

The JI was founded in 1971 independently of the Muslim Brotherhood. At first it was a student movement which concentrated on the imitation of the archetype of the "pious forefathers" and publicly propagated a god-fearing life. Beards, the wearing of veils, and the separation of the sexes were seen as essential for the implementation of an Islamic way of life. Indeed, the books of Sayyid Qutb were mentioned, but initially it was, above all, preaching and proclamation (Arabic: *da'wa*) that were seen as the fitting means for implementing a true Islamic society. Up until 1993, the blind sheik 'Umar 'Abd ar-Rahman (b. 1938) was the spiritual leader and, via his Fatwas (legal opinions), the provider of a basis of justification for activities and stances. In a Fatwa, he sanctioned the assassination of President Sadat in 1981.

Up into the 1980s the group held back from political action, but then they became radicalized and performed several staggering acts of violence. In 1992 the assassination of the secular-oriented intellectual and man of letters Farag Foda was attributed to the group. Foda was known as a critic of the Muslim Brotherhood. In 1997 JI members conducted an assassination attempt on the author and later Nobel Prize winner for literature Naguib Mahfuz, who was badly injured but survived the murderous attempt. In 1995 members of JI made inflammatory remarks against the Koran scholar Professor Nasr Abu Hamid Zaid, who, thereafter and prior to his forced divorce and removal from office, had to hastily leave Egypt. In 1997 the JI conducted an attack on tourists in Luxor, killing 92 people. In 2002 the JI publicly dissociated itself from violence and publicly acknowledged remorse for its actions.

4. *al-Jihad* or *Jama'at al-jihad* (The Jihad or The Community of Jihad-Fighters)

The *Jihad* group, which in turn consisted of several sub-groupings, was founded at the end of the 1970s and was a spin-off of *Jama'at al-Islamiya* (JI). The group's name is connected with a famed writing by 'Abd as-Salam Farraj, *The Neglected Duty* (Arabic: *al-farida al-ga'iba*). It has a wholehearted commitment to militant *Jihad* as the only possible way to bring about the founding of a true Islamic state, a type of primer on modern *Jihadism*. During a military parade, the *Jihad* group and portions of *Jama'at al-Islamiya* undertook a deadly assassination plot on the Egyptian President Anwar al-Sadat on October 6, 1981, the anniversary of the 1973 October War and the crossing of the Suez Canal. Many members of *Jihad* were arrested, and in the 1980s the group established contact with radical movements. In 1998 *Jihad* officially associated itself with Osama bin Laden.

From 1970 to 1980, amnesty was granted to Muslim brothers under President Anwar al-Sadat, who himself is said to have entertained a certain sympathy for the Muslim Brotherhood movement. In 1971, the year in which general amnesty was granted, the movement was officially allowed. As a concession to the Muslim Brotherhood, in 1980 Sadat instituted the *sharia* as the sole source of legislation. Particularly at universities he used the movement as a bulwark against communism and its leftist-oriented adherents, which had been promoted under Nasser but had gone out of style by 1980. The Muslim Brotherhood was, however, not allowed as a political party, since parties based on religious or racist criteria had been forbidden by Sadat. Nevertheless, in recent times numerous candidates from the Muslim Brotherhood, as representatives of other parties such as the conservative-nationalist liberal Wafd party, the workers' party, or the liberals share in the government.

In the 1970s, when the Muslim Brotherhood was free to operate, several small groups of activists associated themselves with it. In part they advocated violence as a means of achieving their goals and were also supported by neighboring Sudanese extremists. Radical wings of the Muslim Brotherhood became increasingly radical and conducted individual attacks. In 1977, at the time when President Sadat started official negotiations with Israel, the movement split and the former members who spun off into their own groups were thought to have committed treason against Islam. Incidentally, in 1979, under the direction of Jimmy Carter, negotiations with Israel led to the Camp David Accords. The development toward radicalization in the group reached its zenith in the assassination of President Anwar al-Sadat at a military parade on October 6, 1981. The assassination was conducted by former members of the Muslim Brotherhood who had moved into the *al-takfir wa-l hijra* ("Excommunication and Exodus") group.

After long years of repression, the Egyptian state recognized that prison, torture, and death had not been effective ways of fighting political Islam and extremism. On the contrary, the brutal persecution of the Muslim Brotherhood by the government had strengthened and accelerated the radicalization of the movement, since, in the eyes of the Muslim brothers, the government had proven its anti-Islamic attitude over against "true Islam." After Anwar al-Sadat's violent death, from 1981 onward, his successor, Hosni Mubarak, primarily attached importance to re-education of, public expressions of remorse toward, and privileges for former radical forces.

An assassination attempt was conducted in 1995 against Hosni Mubarak, not directly by the Muslim Brotherhood but by an ideologically related group. In 1997 there was a severe attack in the city of Luxor; it was intended to bring tourism to a halt and, at the same time, to destabilize the Egyptian state. The result was a renewed wave of arrests of Muslim Brotherhood adherents and a prohibition against all political parties with programs that involved a synthesis of politics and religion.

In 2001 the Muslim Brotherhood distanced itself from the use of violence and attacks, such as those on September 11, 2001, in the USA. It distanced itself as well from Osama bin Laden. All the same, the USA froze accounts in the USA attributable to the Muslim Brotherhood amounting to US$ 43 million.[20] In addition to that, the Muslim Brotherhood felt the effects of various measures taken by the USA in its "war on terror."

---

[20] According to the article "Muslim Brotherhood," In: Roy, Olivier; Sfeir, Antoine (Hg.) The Columbia World Dictionary of Islamism. Columbia University Press: New York, 2007, pp. 235-242, here p. 238.

In recent years reports have surfaced about crises and disputes among different wings of the Muslim Brotherhood. These disputes have to do with the election of successors in the upper echelons of leadership. It has become known that various positions exist in various wings which, in part, see the future of the Brotherhood in pursuit of a more radical, militant line. On the other hand, there are other types of positions that plead for more conciliatory cooperation with the Egyptian government. In addition, there has been a decided distancing of al-Azhar University from the Muslim Brotherhood, which, in the Egyptian context, carries much weight and expresses resistance against the Brotherhood's program of Islamification in Egyptian society.[21]

In 2005, the Muslim Brotherhood in Egypt, with its independent candidates, came away with 88 of 444 seats and in so doing showed itself to be the strongest opposition force in the elections. The Muslim Brotherhood officially professes adherence to democratic and pluralistic notions. Prior to the Egyptian revolution of 2011, the Brotherhood was still officially prohibited, though it was tolerated, in particular as a charity, and it therefore received significant support primarily from the poorer layers of society, i.e., from "all those segments of the population ... which cannot or can barely handle their everyday problems, be they of an economic, social, or cultural variety. Islamic fundamentalism promises them a comprehensive and by comparison simple solution ... They hold out the prospect of economic justice, alleviate social injustices by providing services and secure self-confidence and a foothold through active cooperative efforts."[22] Promises to provide services had a considerable share of the success of the Muslim Brotherhood being elected in 2012 in Egypt.

The ascent and establishment of Islamic movements has not, however, been a phenomenon limited to Egypt. The Muslim Brotherhood gained a foothold in surrounding countries. It fell into a collision course with the government in Syria, while it attempted elsewhere, e.g., in Jordan, to exercise political influence through involvement in government. In most Muslim majority countries, the Muslim Brotherhood has continually been oscillating between being tolerated to experiencing confrontation and

---

[21] According to the summary of the current state of the internal debate of the Muslim Brotherhood in the article "Muslim Brotherhood" in Roy, Olivier; Sfeir, Antoine (eds.) *The Columbia World Dictionary of Islamism*. Columbia University Press: New York, 2007, pp. 235-242, here p. 238.

[22] Steinberg, Guido. *Islamismus und islamistischer Terrorismus im Nahen und Mittleren Osten. Ursachen der Anschläge vom 11. September 2001. Konrad-Adenauer-Stiftung, Zukunftsforum Politik Nr. 39*, St. Augustin: 2002, pp. 27-28.

prohibition, between waves of arrests among the leading figures and attempts to bring them to distance themselves from violence.

However, even when looking beyond the Muslim Brotherhood, the twentieth century has to be seen as the century of political Islam. Numerous movements arose, which, in varying degrees, advocated violence as a means of achieving their goals and were able to exercise political influence. For these movements, it was essentially a matter of warding off western influences, recovering Islam as it was originally practiced in its early years, and bringing about the Islamification of society with the aid of the implementation of *sharia* legislation.

If, at the dawn of the twentieth century, it was the influence of colonial powers in regions shaped by Islam that provided the justification to develop the movement of political Islam to reinvigorate and purify Islam, in the middle of the twentieth century, it was the traumatic Arab loss in the 1967 Six-Day War and the breakdown of "Nasserism" which provoked the ascent of political Islam. In addition, in the second half of the twentieth century, there was growing dissatisfaction because of a lack of opportunities for many hundreds of thousands of university graduates in the face of a generally insufficient manner of coping with the challenges of modernity and a perennially weak infrastructure.

There exists a group of social, political, and economic transitions that are commonly attributed to the west and which contribute to a high level of dissatisfaction among the broad population that form the social background for the appeal of the Muslim Brotherhood. This includes a reduction in government subsidies that have fallen away because of dropping oil revenues, the Second Gulf War and its catastrophic economic consequences for the neighboring regions, declining support from the United States and the disintegrating Soviet Union, the economic downturn brought on by globalization, corruption of the elite, and much restricted civil rights and liberties when compared with the situation in the west. In connection with the Second Gulf War, as well as with the campaigns in Afghanistan and Iraq, the intensified feeling was that an undermining and destruction of Islam was afoot with the aid of weapons, commerce, and the importation of western (non)culture, all serving to humiliate Muslim majority countries and their people.

The high points of the movement were the outbreak of (even if shaped by Shi'ism) the Islamic Revolution in 1979, the displacement of the PLO by Hamas at the end of the 1980s, the attempted seizure of power by the FIS (*Front Islamique du Salut*) in Algeria in 1992 and the ensuing civil war, the Sudanese military dictatorship under Hassan al-Turabi, and the conflict of the Afghani mujahideen against the Soviet Army beginning in 1979.[23]

F. The Muslim Brotherhood as an international movement

There are voices which primarily style the Muslim Brotherhood as an endeavor that has secretly built up a parallel economic empire.[24] Others view it, above all, as an ideological service provider to the disappointed and frequently impoverished masses within societies shaped by Islam.

The Muslim Brotherhood has, in the meantime, spread to all parts of the earth. According to their own reports, the Muslim Brotherhood exists in approximately 70 countries – among them Iraq, Libya, Tunisia, Algeria, Sudan, the Gulf states, Saudia Arabia, Lebanon, Palestine, Yemen, and Europe as well – and is dedicated to its original goals: social work and the propagation and implementation of a comprehensive, political form of Islam. For a long time it has been one of the most influential political and welfare movements which functions worldwide by operating supermarket chains, slaughterhouses, hospitals, financial networks, mosque-related relief organizations, branches of social service, religious schools, and other facilities and positioning its members in the corridors of power in the army, parliament, and society.

For the underprivileged, destitute layers of society, who see themselves as neglected by the powerful people of their country or altogether powerless, the Muslim Brotherhood is, above all, a relief organization which promised to erect justice. An extensive movement such as the Muslim Brotherhood gives the middle class a sense of belonging to an influential organization that can be used for one's own advancement. In this way, the Muslim Brotherhood produces a bond between the various classes of society and quite practically promotes the unity that it propagates.

G. Jordan

Jordan is one of the countries with one of the more influential forms of the Muslim Brotherhood in the Middle East, where the movement was

---

[23] Guido Steinberg. *Der Islamismus im Niedergang?* In. *Islamismus. Texte zur Inneren Sicherheit.* Bundesministerium des Innern. Berlin 2004/2, pp. 19-42, here pp. 30-31 with reference to Gilles Kepel. *Das Schwarzbuch des Jihad.* Piper: München, 2002, p. 89ff.

[24] So, for instance, the article "Muslim Brotherhood" in Roy, Olivier; Sfeir, Antoine (eds.) *The Columbia World Dictionary of Islamism.* Columbia University Press: New York, 2007, pp. 235-242, here p. 238.

founded in Amman in 1936. In 1948 it was recognized as a non-profit organization. The Muslim Brotherhood has exercised lasting influence in Jordan, especially via the ministries for religious affairs and education and its good cooperation in government circles and with the Hashemite royal house. These good contacts were attributable to the fact that, among other reasons, beginning in the middle of the 1960s, many of the Ba'ath party members in Syria who were persecuted members of the Muslim Brotherhood fled to Jordan. In 1992 the Muslim Brotherhood founded its own political party, the IAF (Islamic Action Front). In 1993 the Muslim Brotherhood lost the majority of its parliamentary seats. In 2001 there were some short-lived conflicts with the royal house and King Abdullah II. However, in 2002 the Muslim Brotherhood named a new leader of the IAF with good relations to the royal house. Since that time, the Muslim Brotherhood in Jordan appears to have adjusted to a moderate course.

H. Syria

In Syria as well, the Muslim Brotherhood founded an organization early on; in 1938 it emerged for the first time via activities by students who had returned to Syria after studying in Egypt. Officially it was founded by Mustafa as-Siba'i in 1947 in Homs. In the 1940s and 1950s, the Muslim Brotherhood canvassed for adherents in opposition to the Ba'ath and communist parties, finding them among traditional believers and the working class. However, it very rapidly fell into a foundational conflict with the government. In 1963 the nationalist-socialist oriented Ba'ath Party came to power and began to combat the Muslim Brotherhood as a radical opposition movement. In particular, from 1976 onward, the Muslim Brotherhood was seen as an enemy of the Assad government, which had come to power in 1971, and against which the Brotherhood conducted attacks. President Hafiz al-Assad is said to have been personally attacked by them in an assassination attempt. In 1980 the movement was officially banned, and the years 1981 and 1982 mark the high point of the clash between the government and the Muslim Brotherhood. With a large contingent, the military marched into the city of Hama, which the Muslim Brotherhood had declared to be an independent "City of the Muslim Brotherhood" that no longer stood under the Ba'ath Party government. Allegedly, in the government's attempt to completely destroy the Muslim Brotherhood, between 10,000 and 30,000 were killed. Many fled to foreign Arab countries and to Europe, and others were thrown into prison.

In the mid-1990s, there was a certain rapprochement between the Muslim Brotherhood and the government. Bashir al-Assad granted prisoners amnesty, and in 2001 the Muslim Brotherhood officially declared its renunciation of violence. Since that time a reestablishment of the movement is said to have taken place; it enjoys societal and political influence in Syria. In 2005 the Syrian Muslim Brotherhood signed the "Damascus Declaration," in which they, along with other opposition groups, advocated the establishment of a representative democracy.

On the one hand, the influence of the Muslim Brotherhood is publicly ensured today through its participation in government. On the other hand, its influence is privately ensured via its various organizations and associated organizations. Most members keep quiet about their membership, spreading rumors and false information.

I. Europe

The Muslim Brotherhood is firmly established in Europe. However, it has to grapple with competing movements such as Indian-Pakistani, Saudi, and Turkish groups, which likewise strive for influence among Europe's Muslims. In part, it rules over directly related associations, in part over associated organizations which spread the Muslim Brotherhood ideology. An example is the European Council for Fatwa and Research (ECFR). In part there is healthy cooperation with associated organizations such as the Saudi organization World Assembly of Muslim Youth (WAMY), in which members of the Muslim Brotherhood hold leading positions.

The Muslim Brotherhood's focus in Europe lies in Germany, France, Switzerland, Great Britain, and Belgium. The European umbrella organization of the Muslim Brotherhood is the Federation of Islamic Organizations in Europe (FIOE), headquartered in Leicester, Great Britain. It is said to be primarily supported with funds from the Gulf states.

In 1958, with the aid of the Saudi Prince Faisal, an "Islamic Center" was founded in Geneva, Switzerland, under the leadership of Said Ramadan (1926-1994), the personal secretary and son-in-law of Hassan al-Banna, who was the founder of the Muslim Brotherhood. Said Ramadan maintained good contacts with Sayyid Qutb. In the years 1949-1954, Said Ramadan was the head of the Muslim Brotherhood in Egypt and thereafter lived in Jerusalem. The Islamic Center in Geneva became a place of refuge for the members of the Muslim Brotherhood who had fled from Egypt. The Muslim Brotherhood in France is represented by the "Union des Organisations Islamiques de France" (UOIF) and in Italy by the "Unione delle Comunità ed Organizzazioni Islamiche" (ECOI).

In the meantime, an elderly Sunni scholar, Sheikh Yusuf al-Qaradawi (born 1926), is an influential personality in Europe; he is a figurehead and a type of a unofficial spiritual leader of the movement. Allegedly he is perhaps the most influential legal scholar, Mufti (an interpreter or expounder of Islamic law who issues legal opinions), and Islamic publicist at the moment. He affirms the corporal disciplining of disobedient wifes and defends suicide attacks in Palestine. He upholds the beating of homosexuals, the execution of adulterers and apostates, and at least till 2001, female circumcision (Female Genital Mutilation, or FGM). In 2004 Al-Qaradawi founded the International Association of Muslim Scholars (IAMS) in London. In 1996 he co-founded the European Council for Fatwa and Research (ECFR), and since that time he has been the council's chairman. The ECFR is closely tied to the Muslim Brotherhood. With its internet portals "www.islamonline.net" and "www.onislam.net" as well as the program "The Sharia and Life" (Arabic: *al-sharia wa l-haya*) on al-Jazeera, al-Qaradawi reaches an audience of millions in the Middle East and Europe.

Beyond such individual personalities, the Muslim Brotherhood exercises influence via many of its personages in positions of leadership, who are in well- established posts in Europe as contact persons for church and state, as dialog and negotiating partners, and as political advisors.

"Muslims are obligated to continue jihad, which will bring about the collapse of western civilization and the ascent of Muslim civilization upon its ruins."

J. Germany

"Why should we not take advantage of western laws, if they open a way for us to pursue our goals?" (A speaker of the Muslim Brotherhood)

Germany is an important center for the worldwide activities of the Muslim Brotherhood. In the 1950s and 1960s, thousands of Muslim students left the Middle East to pursue studies at German universities. They desired to sidestep persecution by repressive regimes and, at the same time, to earn degrees that are highly reputable internationally. Germany has especially welcomed Syrian and Egyptian students, whose governments stood on the side of the Soviet Union.

The "Islamische Gemeinschaft in Deutschland" or IGD (Islamic Community in Germany), which was founded in 1958, is supposed to support the influence of the Muslim Brotherhood in Germany.[25] It is said to have approximately 1,250 members and is a member of the Federation of Islamic Organizations in Europe (FIOE), which was founded in 1989. From 1958-1968 its president was Said Ramadan, the co-founder of the Muslim

---

[25] Grundmann, Johannes. *Islamische Internationalisten. Strukturen und Aktivitäten der Muslimbruderschaft und der islamischen Weltliga.* Reichert: Wiesbaden, 2005, p. 59.

World League as well as the personal secretary of Hassan al-Banna. The Pakistani Fazal Yazdani became the successor in 1968, and following him, the Syrian Ghaleb Himmat. Himmat was one of the founders of the Bank al-Taqwa, the bank of the Muslim Brotherhood. It has financed several Islamic centers in Europe and, at least since the middle of the 1990s, is said to have conducted money laundering. The Bank al-Taqwa is also said to have supported various extremist and terrorist groups, such as al Qaeda, Hamas, the FIS, and the Tunisian branch of the Muslim Brotherhood, an-Nahda. The IGD is headquartered at the Islamic Center of Munich.

Himmat's successor was Ibrahim al-Zayat, during the years 2002-2010. al-Zayat always contested that he belonged to the Muslim Brotherhood. According to press reports, he was recently being investigated for membership in a criminal organization on counts of fraud, money laundering, and misuse of donated funds.

Additionally, the Muslim Brotherhood has other organizations or spin-offs with its former members in Germany, such as the Islamische Bund Palästinas (IBP) – al-Aqsa e.V. (Islamic Federation for Palestine – al-Aqsa, a registered association). with a few hundred members; the Islamische Heilsfront or FIS (Islamic Salvation Front); and the Bewaffnete Islamische Gruppe or GIA (Armed Islamic Group), including its spin-off, the Salafiyya-Gruppe für die Mission und den Kampf or GSPC (Groupe Salafiste pour la Prédication et le Combat/Salafiyya Group for Preaching and Combat), with fewer than 100 members.

In 2001, during the investigation of a Muslim Brotherhood activist in Campione, Switzerland, a document, "The Project," was found. It described the Muslim Brotherhood's plan to permeate Europe with the ideology of the Muslim Brotherhood. They would seek to do this via targeted deception, the erection of an Islamic intellectual movement, and the control and surveillance of western media reports through founding schools, keeping thoughts of jihad awake in the minds of Muslims in the west, and stoking hatred against the west in order to promote the implementation of Islamic values. Unfortunately, one cannot say that the Muslim Brotherhood has remained unsuccessful in its plan.

K. The Muslim Brotherhood today

The Muslim Brotherhood today is a worldwide, very well-networked, financially well-endowed Sunni movement with politico-societal influence via committees working on political co-determination (parliaments); influential scholars who also release statements (on the internet and television, in books, and in the media); and administration of Muslim centers (Munich, among others) and financial and personal networks. Within the movement there appear to be conflicts between the more militant wings, conservatives, and moderate progressives, with the more progressive wings desiring increased cooperation with governments.

In Egypt the Muslim Brotherhood moved along a fine line between toleration and restriction for decades. Before it came to power for about a year between 2012 and 2013 after the Arab Revolution in Egypt, the government sensed that it is too powerful, the closing of facilities was threatened, their preachers were banned from speaking, and their accounts were confiscated. The Muslim Brotherhood was not be able to be founded and operate as a separate party, since Egyptian law on political parties offered the regime far-ranging authority – especially such authority that allows it religious grounds – upon which to issue prohibitions. The result was that Muslim Brothers could only run for office as independent candidates or under the mantle of another party.

> *"Jihad will lead to the destruction of western civilization and replace it with Islam, which will rule the world" (the former supreme leader of the Muslim Brotherhood, Mahdi Akif, in 2007).*

L. And the movement's successes?

Because in numerous countries the social space has not been filled by the state or other institutions, the Muslim Brotherhood has, above all, enjoyed success through its wide-ranging social work. It offers Koran courses and sporting events; opens kindergartens, schools, clinics, and even emergency medical facilities and hospitals; offers legal counsel and job fairs; gives food to the unemployed; offers disaster relief; and cares for refugees. In this way the Muslim Brotherhood sets up a parallel society in which it passes on its worldview and its view of the enemy. On the other hand, it enjoys high social acclaim as a countermovement against a corrupt and often passive state. The currently envisaged hanging of about 700 members of the Muslim Brotherhood will additionally give them a martyrs' status in the eyes of their adherents. At the same time, many new sympathizers are won via this practical type of missions work. The fact that the group provides such necessary services prevented it being forbidden by the state.[26] In the process, the organizations affiliated with the Muslim Brotherhood finance themselves via commercial enterprises, donations, and their own

---

[26] According to Ivesa Lübben. "Die ägyptische Muslimbruderschaft – Auf dem Weg zur politischen Partei" Albrecht, Holger; Köhler, Kevin (eds.) *Politischer Islam im Vorderen Orient. Zwischen Sozialbewegung, Opposition und Widerstand. Weltreligionen im Wandel 5*. Nomos: Baden-Baden, 2008, pp. 75-97, here p. 81.

banks, which individuals, in turn, trust with their deposits and, on the basis of Islamic principles followed, hold to be more reliable than state banks. Additionally, Islamistic and terrorist movements receive support from private donors, states, and large state organizations from some countries in the Middle East.

The movement of political Islam is not only a social movement. It simultaneously attempts to operate financially independently via its economic enterprises. Through its various stakeholders and institutions, it attempts to influence the public, e.g., in employee committees, unions, and universities, as well as through politics. Up to the upheavels in the Middle East, it aimed to either participate in elections with the aid of other political parties,[27] to be in parliaments via its own parties, to be represented as participants in coalition governments (Iraq, Algeria, Somalia, Sudan), or, elsewhere, to operate as banned underground organizations (Libya, Syria, Tunisia).

The Muslim Brotherhood has also been successful in the establishment of an active worldwide movement of mutual support which is financially strong and well-networked, exercises ongoing influence, and is, in part, socially and politically acknowledged. A true recasting of society into an Islamic one has never been achieved by the Muslim Brotherhood, and except for the brief presidency of Mohammed Morsi in Egypt, it has not it been able to achieve a parliamentary majority or to take over the government. If one were to mention Iran as an exception for an Islamic state, it is to be noted that it is not ruled by the Muslim Brotherhood. Rule by the Muslim Brotherhood would presumably also be rather difficult, since the Muslim Brotherhood (on this point the Muslim Brotherhood resembles similar movements of Islamism and Jihadism) has until now not formulated any comprehensive state, economic, and social theory for the establishment of an alternative society. Rather, it has concentrated on particular aspects, e.g., how hospitals are operated. In this way the Muslim Brotherhood is an extraordinarily large and influential political power and has a vast number of members, all without being allowed to exist as an official party.

In no country – up to the short-lived takeover of power in Egypt in 2012 – has the Muslim Brotherhood achieved an overthrow of the government, and it has never come close to establishing a caliphate. However, the Muslim Brotherhood has been successful in its attempt to permeate the societies of the Middle East as well as Muslim communities in Europe with its

---

[27] According to Albrecht, Holger; Köhler, Kevin (eds.) *Politischer Islam im Vorderen Orient. Zwischen Sozialbewegung, Opposition und Widerstand. Weltreligionen im Wandel 5.* Nomos: Baden-Baden, 2008, p. 13.

ideas of political Islam, according to which no form of government, will of the people, or way of life which deviates from the *sharia* finds justification. There are repeated examples where the Muslim Brotherhood has exacerbated inflammatory centers of conflict and has even conducted media and propaganda efforts that have worked to stoke issues in a way that does not promote integration and does not help to bring about peaceful coexistence between Muslims and non-Muslims.[28]

M. The problematic nature of political Islam

The problematic nature of political Islam does not lie in its theological point of view. The idea that one has the only correct interpretation of Islam does not make a movement radical. On the contrary, this sort of theological absolutism is something political Islam shares with other Islamic groups and, by the way, with at least the other monotheistic world religions and numerous additional worldviews. The problematic nature of the Muslim Brotherhood lies in its political program. Generally speaking, this is the problematic nature of all movements of political Islam. They demonstrate a principial readiness to use violence to implement their goals or, at least, not to dissociate themselves from the use of violence by groups that are ideologically related. Furthermore, their problematic nature is also found in their totalitarianism and their dealings with minorities and those who think differently, indeed even with other Muslims who do not share their views. If political Islam is lifting up as the norm for all times a *sharia*-defined legal and societal order and the early Islamic society of a tribal and, in part, nomadically shaped body politic or community of the seventh century A.D. Arabian Peninsula, the result has to be a rejection of all the rights and freedoms which contradict this postulated ideal picture of society.

1. Dealing with those who think differently

The sole identity that an individual under the flag of political Islam can accept is that of a believing Muslim according to the political interpretation; otherwise the individual has only a limited, temporary, or, in the worst case, non-existent right to exist. Never, however, could Muslims and non-Muslims, Jews and Christians, the non-religious and people with other beliefs, men and women, Sunnis and Shiites, believers and atheists have equal rights and liberties under such a societal model. Women in an Islam-based body politic can only enjoy limited rights, since the traditional inter-

---

[28] According to, for instance, its role in connection with the so-called "cartoon controversy." Jytte Klausen. *The Cartoons that shook the World.* Yale University Press: New Haven, 2009, pp. 103ff.

pretation of the *sharia,* to which political Islam is doubtless committed, grants them limited rights under inheritance and marital law, limited rights under divorce and child custody law, and limited rights in witness-related law. At the same time, the equal recognition of minorities (including Muslim minorities), atheists, and converts is decidedly rejected.

Islamic fundamentalism's claim that its establishment of a religiously based rule will bring all people peace and justice appears to be unrealistic, particularly in those countries that have made it their declared aim to be to fully implement the *sharia.* Never have societies which, for example, have applied the corporal punishment of the *sharia* (e.g., Iran or the northern states of Nigeria) experienced increases in prosperity, peace, and affluence. Rather, the opposite has been the case: there is arbitrariness and cruelty, contempt for minorities and the defenseless, oppression of those who hold other religious or moral convictions (based solely up the testimony of Muslims, frequently observed in Pakistan), and the loss of rights to freedom and equality. Indeed the following could generally be noted: The decline in civil rights and liberties especially equal rights, the persecution of critics, and generally a decline in constitutionality and the functioning social order.

2. Totalitarianism instead of a separation of powers

If the Koran and the Sunna are the sole foundation and guideline not only for faith, but also for society, jurisprudence, and politics, in such a society there can be no separation of powers and with that, no constitutional legality or court of appeal against injustice on the side of the state and in all the organs under its control.

In this model for explaining the world, the caliphate appears to be the only thinkable model for government and authority. The caliph is the spiritual and political ruler, legislator, and supreme judge, as well as guard over the implementation of the *sharia.* The *sharia* contains the application of corporal punishment, including lashings, stoning, and the amputation of the hand and/or the foot as the just punishment for adultery, theft, or extramarital relationships. According to the classical interpretation, the *sharia* applies the death penalty against apostates. Apostates do not have any opportunity to appeal to any state or religious level of jurisdiction or constitutional court regarding civil rights and liberties. A state under the *sharia*, according to the model of the Muslim Brotherhood, cannot be a state that accords civil rights and liberties, rights of equality, and religious rights. The absence of a separation of powers prohibits freedom of opinion, civil rights and liberties, equal rights, self-determination, and the choice to have no religion; freedom to conduct research, produce art, and pursue science, as well as the unhindered exchange of political or religious convictions. There is no freedom to form the political will and no possibility of free elections and sovereignty of the people. A secular-based political order, enlightenment, and opinion pluralism can find no justification and at best, for pragmatic reasons, are temporarily tolerated until ways open to exercise influence by implementing a caliphate.

3. Contempt for others, how the enemy is seen, and violence

Political Islam's system of theories additionally conveys drastic pictures of the enemy, i.e., of "the west," of "Zionists," of "crusaders," as well as pictures of "Jews" and "Christians." Through its ideological justification, it affords an impetus to far-reaching anti-Semitism. According to political Islam, a life worth living and a just society can only come about in a theocratic state that is under the *sharia*. This is not possible elsewhere. Groups with people who believe otherwise are disapproved of, and their legal system and way of life are tolerated but not acknowledged to be of equal value.

Additionally, there is the problematic nature of a frequently unclear boundary between violence and political overthrow and the justification of "defense" of the Islamic community, e.g., via suicide bombings in Palestine. A basic revision of thinking does not appear to be foreseeable, even if today the Muslim Brotherhood appears to be primarily relying on exercising political influence instead of conducting militant attacks. In the final instance, the Muslim Brotherhood's ideology is also aimed at using coercion or even violence in order to establish the "ideal society." In this way, it offers the ideological substructure for almost all of modernity's movements of political and jihadist Islam, including their spokesmen.

Finally, political Islam offers an ideal breeding ground for the advocacy and exercise of violence through deriving an exalted view of history from the past. Because it recognizes Mohammed's actions against his enemies to be a direct role model for the present time and declares his militant activities as a warlord to be legitimate, political Islam offers a historical justification for the exercise of violence. Some Islamists assert that the use of violence is merely a temporary necessity in order to establish what will be, in the end, a more peaceful and just society. That Hassan al-Banna, one of the 'founding fathers' of what is today the most important movement of political Islam, never personally resorted to means of violence yet did not delimit his teaching on the complete implementation of Islam and the problematic nature of jihad and the exercise of violence, demonstrates with his own words the duty upon all Muslims to also follow Mohammed in his "striving in the path of God" (Arabic: *jihad*). It is beside the point that not all Islamists resort to violence. Principally, it is not an effective step to separate political Islam from violence and the advocacy of violence. Indeed, many Islamists condemn attacks on "the innocent" while not, however, condemning a "defensive war" against "the occupying forces," e.g., in Palestine (such as Yusuf al-Qaradawi).[29]

Hassan al-Banna on Jihad

"Jihad is an obligation from Allah on every Muslim and cannot be ignored nor evaded. Allah has ascribed great importance to jihad and has made the reward of the martyrs and the fighters in His way a splendid one. Only those who have acted similarly and who have modeled themselves upon the martyrs in their performance of jihad can join them in this reward. Furthermore, Allah has specifically honored the Mujahideen with certain exceptional qualities, both spiritual and practical, to benefit them in this world and the next. Their pure blood is a symbol of victory in this world and the mark of success and felicity in the world to come.

Those who can only find excuses, however, have been warned of extremely dreadful punishments and Allah has described them with the most unfortunate of names. He has reprimanded them for their cowardice and lack of spirit, and castigated them for their weakness and truancy. In this world, they will be surrounded by dishonor and in the next they will be surrounded by the fire from which they shall not escape though they may possess much wealth. The weaknesses of abstention and evasion of jihad are regarded by Allah as one of the major sins, and one of the seven sins that guarantee failure.

Islam is concerned with the question of jihad and the drafting and the mobilization of the entire Umma into one body to defend the right cause with all its strength [more] than any other ancient or modern system of living, whether religious or civil. The verses of the Koran and the Sunna of Muhammad (peace be upon him) are overflowing with all these noble ideals and they summon people in general (with the most eloquent expression and the clearest exposition) to jihad, to warfare, to the armed forces, and all means of land and sea fighting. We shall not go into exhaustive detail but rather will offer you some Koranic verses and Ahaadeeth [hadith] below as examples since we only wish to show a glimpse of the Islamic message on jihad.

---

[29] According to Bettina Gräf. "Yusuf al-Qaradawi und die Bildung einer 'globalen islamischen Autorität'" http://de.qantara.de/webcom/show_article.php/_c-468/_nr-323/i.html (accessed February 22, 2010).

Furthermore, we will not delve into the explanation of the Koranic verses or Ahaadeeth. You will recognize by the purity of language, the clarity of exposition, the lucidity of ideas and the force of spirituality that explanations and clarifications are not required ... [30]

---

[30] Hassan al-Banna. *Jihad – a comprehensive view*. Quoted from: http://www.2mus lims.com/directory/Detailed/226270.shtml (accessed February 22, 2010).

III. What available solutions could defuse political Islam?

Can political Islam be subdued? Since the causes in the home countries shaped by Islam are manifold and complex, simple solutions are not foreseeable. Caution is required to avoid the hasty assumption that individual movements, which are offshoots of their mother organizations in the Middle East and have declared their support of democracy and constitutionality, have effectively separated themselves from the political Islam of their countries of origin.

Can political Islam be prevented from gaining ground in Europe, so that because of the influence of political Islam, jihadism does not grow even more in Europe? Are current integration and aid programs, cooperation with non-political forces, enhanced language promotions, and eased naturalization procedures sufficient to effectively prevent a radicalization of the Muslim community? Are security measures the only way to protect western societies? What else can be done?

A. Muslims in Germany – have they remained foreigners, or have they arrived home?

According to a survey conducted for the *ARD Morgenmagazin* television program by dimap (*Das Institut für Markt- und Politikforschung*), an institute for market and political research, only 22% of German citizens "*have no problem with the Muslim faith;*" 39% express "*a little bit of worry;*" and 36% have "*extensive worries about an expansion of Islam.*"[31] In other words, 75% of German citizens are characterized by fear and worry with respect to Islam. However, even among Muslim immigrants, a high percentage have remained at somewhat of a distance to Germany, but 36% of Muslims in Germany feel more closely tied to Germany than to their country of origin. More interesting still are the responses among Muslims with German passports: only 51% feel stronger ties to Germany than to their family countries of origin, even though most did not grow up outside Germany.[32] Only 22% of Muslims living in Hamburg and 25% in Berlin view themselves as Germans. However, – and this is much more striking – only 11% of Muslims in both cities indicate that they are seen by others as

---

[31] A large Majority of Germans are worried about Islam. *Die Welt*, December 12, 2009, p. 4.

[32] *Muslimisches Leben in Deutschland*, published by the Federal Office for Migration and Refugees. Nürnberg: 2009, p. 338.

Germans![33] Of those asked across Germany, approximately half of the Muslim population in Germany feels disliked by Germans.[34]

B. The way from political Islam to jihadism

Islamists who, over the long term, want to turn the country from a democracy into a caliphate state are not all that is problematic for the security of Germany or Europe. It is those who also make the additional step from political Islam to jihadism and radicalize in the middle of western societies. How does this happen? And for what reasons?

At first, an obvious supposition is that whoever affiliates with a jihadist group does so because he interprets the Koran "literally" or is particularly devout. However, all available studies that apply to Europe contradict this assumption. The typical new initiate in a jihadist group does not indicate a particularly religious past or interest. Indeed, even when considered in a global framework, virtually all leading jihadists have enjoyed insufficient or a total lack of theological training.[35] Meager theological knowledge, not a too intensive preoccupation with the Koran and Islamic theology, makes a person susceptible to radicalization. Without a corresponding instructional substructure that claims Mohammed's *jihad* against his enemies in the seventh century A.D. now has to be put into action against the west in a war of terrorism, the "sword verses" are only historical accounts. Admittedly, it is a number of jihadist groups which are providing this ideological substructure by turning an historical account into a principle of action today.

Although it could be obvious at the outset, jihadists are not psychopaths who have experienced brainwashing and who now obey orders as will-less remote- controlled robots. As a general rule, they do not suffer from any recognizable mental confusion. At least the ringleaders of the movements are generally neither poor nor uneducated; rather, they come from the as-

---

[33]   According to the results of the survey *Muslims in Europe: A Report on 11 EU cities des Londoner Open Society Institute* (OSI) (http://www.ufuq.de/news blog/605-studie-qmuslims-in-europe-a-report-on-11-eu-citiesq) (accessed December 19, 2009).

[34]   Katrin Brettfeld; Peter Wetzels. *Muslime in Deutschland. Eine Studie des Bundesinnenministeriums zu Integration, Integrationsbarrieren, Religion und Einstellungen zu Demokratie, Rechtsstaat und politisch-religiös motivierter Gewalt*. Hamburg: 2007, p. 109.

[35]   According to, among others a study by the British government: Pursue, *Prevent, Protect, Prepare. Countering the terrorist threat: The UK Government's strategy*, p. 42 (http://www.fco.gov.uk/resources/en/pdf/3849543/pppp-strategy.pdf) (accessed December 21, 2009).

piring middle class, with good prospects for lasting careers and societal success.

Indeed, there are a number of mosques in Germany which are known for being a breeding ground for radical teaching. However, the preferred and most frequent locations for radicalization are not mosques, especially not the mosques within the DITIB (*Dachverband Türkish-Islamische Union der Anstalt für Religion e.V.* or Umbrella Organization of the Turkish and Islamic Union for the Institute of Religion) or the mosques with particularly high minarets. Rather, it is more the informal meeting places which lie remote from the mosques, such as bookstores, international call shops, schools, universities, and, increasingly nowadays, prisons.

For a longer period of time it was the internet and the way it could make global appeals for participation in *jihad*, its directions for constructing explosives, and its glorification of commitment to martyrdom that were quite considered some of the most dangerous instigators of radicalization. This is not quite correct. The internet has not been shown to be an actual instigator of radicalization in 99% of the jihadist biographies. To be sure, the internet acts as an accelerator of the process of radicalization in the sense that it makes necessary information (i.e., technical information) accessible to those who have decided for *jihad*. However, the internet alone does not provide the defining moment. An individual does not become an attacker simply because he sits in front of his computer and watches how a bomb is constructed. In almost every individual case of jihadist attacks, there are detectable contacts to a group and/or a spiritual leader or leading operational figure that were more important than internet use.36 The determination to finally take the step to action normally arises via a necessary group dynamic in some sort of forum and not independently thereof.[37]

C. Pathways to radicalization

Numerous studies, which on the basis of all available data in Europe and around the world provide information about planned as well as conducted jihadist attacks, come to the same conclusions with respect to their analyses of radicalization. One of these studies, by the New York Police De-

---

[36] This is also the result to which a 2008 Europe-wide study by the European Commission's Change Institute in London came: *Studies into violent radicalisation; Lot 2. The beliefs, ideologies and narratives*, p. 4. (http://ec.europa.eu/justice_home/fsj/terrorism/prevention/docs/ec_radicalisation_study_on_ideology_and_narrative_en.pdf) (accessed December 21 2009).

[37] Also according to Oliver Roy. "Al-Qaeda: A True Global Movement" in Rik Coolsaet. *Jihadi Terrorism and the Radicalisation Challenge in Europe*. Ashgate: Aldershot, 2008, pp. 109-114, here p. 112.

partment, entitled "Radicalization in the West: The Homegrown Threat"[38] and based on available information up to 2007, summarizes the individual steps to radicalization.

1. The antecedent to radicalization

The first step in pre-radicalization touches the rather non-religious, inconspicuous aspirant, who is open to new things. The typical participant tends not to have an intensive criminal record, is educated, male, most often married, and frequently the father of more than one child. Converts who feel ostracized by society and are looking for an intensive new place where they can belong are also considered endangered subjects; some 25% of all jihadists are converts. The more isolated and more rigidly structured the aspirant, the more susceptible he is to the jihadist worldview. He views himself as in a society that does not provide him a place. He subjectively views himself as someone who is scorned, and he walls himself off from society by retreating and becoming a member of a jihadist group. In his biography, one immigrant from an Indian-Pakistani background in Great Britain described his pre-radical phase in a typical way with the following words: *"I was 16 years old and did not have a single white friend. My world consisted exclusively of Asians, who were all Muslims. That was my Great Britain."39*

Two groups of people in Europe are susceptible when it comes to possible radicalization in a jihadist group.

a) The first group includes the student under 35 years of age who first immigrates to Europe as an adult for his studies. After a relatively short period of time in Europe, he absorbs some radical thinking or has come to Europe with such thinking. In Europe he is withdrawn from an environment that is laid out as a collective society and is frequently very lonely. He is an outsider and can neither come to grips with the freedom and opportunities nor with the anonymity and missing solidarity in his new environment. An example is the Egyptian cultural studies scholar Hamed Abdul-Samad, who emphatically illustrates his phase of loss of orientation as a student in Germany in his autobiographical narrative *Mein Abschied vom Himmel (My Departure from Heaven)*.[40] For him his homelessness and feeling of being an unwanted alien element in German society almost be-

---

[38]   http://www.nypdshield.org/public/SiteFiles/documents/NYPD_Report-Radicalization_in_the_West.pdf (accessed December 22, 2009).

[39]   Ed Husain. *The Islamist. Why I joined radical Islam in Britain, what I saw inside and why I left*. Penguin Books: London, 2007, p. 35.

[40]   Hamed Abdel-Samad. *Mein Abschied vom Himmel. Aus dem Leben eines Muslims in Deutschland*. Köln: Fackelträger, 2009.

came a building block for his own radicalization: *"Young Muslims feel themselves drawn to militant groups because they offer them acceptance and love and security, and they provide the feeling of being part of a project. In contrast, they receive the feeling from German society as well as from traditional Islamic organizations that they are a problem."*[41] For this reason Abdul-Samad makes a plea for a culture of trust and of bridge-building to people. This is because *"it is not enough to get rid of extremists, because then they really become all the more radicalized."*[42]

b) The second susceptible group is comprised of sons – nowadays frequently even daughters – from middle-class families in the second or third generation of immigrants. They have grown up in Europe but have the distinct feeling that they will never be accepted as locals. They often enjoy little participation in societal matters and view themselves as losers in modernity.

Several studies conducted in the USA indicate that the deep cultural, societal, and economic gap between immigrants of the second and third generations and the majority of the population leads to intensive frustration and the feeling of exclusion. A strong feeling of isolation and denied acceptance as well as the sense of never belonging appear to be significant factors for these adherents on the way to radicalization, as expressed by a youth from Hamburg: *"I was born here, have German citizenship, completed my university entrance degree, and I am now studying. I am a member of a political party and regularly donate blood – what more do I have to do to be accepted as a German?"*[43]

While in search of a place to belong, the "domestic outsider" is especially open to offers of friendship and acceptance. The friendship and acceptance in a jihadist group are all the more intensive since other members find themselves in a similar situation. To arrive and be accepted, to find like-minded people, and with that, to reconstruct a piece of what an individual is accustomed to in a closely knit Muslim family culture make the aspirant open to taking on the worldview of the group.

Immigration in itself appears for many young Muslims to be a significant time of susceptibility to jihadist movements. In many jihadist groups, 80-85% of the members are either themselves immigrants, are the de-

---

41 "'Verfluchte Freiheit.' Ein Gespräch mit dem Kulturwissenschaftler Hamed Abdel-Samad" in: *ufuq* Nr. 15/Dezember 2009, p. 7 (http://ufuq.de/newsblog/607-verfluchte-freiheit-ein-gespraech-mit-hamed-abdel-samad) (accessed December 21, 2009).

42 Ibid.

43 Julia Gerlach. *Zwischen Pop und Dschihad. Muslimische Jugendliche in Deutschland.* Lizenzausgabe Bundeszentrale für politische Bildung: Bonn, 2006, p. 218.

scendants of immigrants, or live in the diaspora. In any event they are not in their country of origin. This is a terrifyingly high number![44]

Whoever strongly interprets life in the diaspora as a defeat, as humiliation, as something marked with discrimination and continuing frustration may very well in the end find his meaning in fighting against society. The lack of opportunities produces additional retreat, and additional retreat produces fewer and fewer opportunities. It is a vicious cycle. If a personal role model or a number of friends are able to convince the lonely, uprooted individual that in this unjust, godless society it is every person's responsibility to fight with *jihad* in order to reshape society into a just form, the discrimination that has been experienced is, on the one hand, magnified, and, at the same time, prospects for bringing about a change to the depressive circumstances are also brought into view. A remaining factor is the way the media report about Islam in a biased manner, as the motor of terrorism, which makes the fight appear to be a justified defensive move.

2. The identification phase

Along with entrance into the group, the participant receives emotional attention, a task among brothers and sisters, a new sense of belonging, respect, and dignity. This has nothing to do with an academic or theological discussion, system of theories, or some sort of balanced comparison of different interpretations of Islam.

Very frequently the aspirant falls into a group where he already has family or friendly ties. In part, there may be long-standing connections that are so strong that they offer firm support in an environment of rejection and uncertainty. This is particularly true in times of economic, societal, political, or personal crisis that can arise through the loss of a job, the death of a relative, or an experience of discrimination. In a number of cases, the candidate is also offered the possibility of marriage within this circle.

If the aspirant has allied himself with the group and developed reliable and sound friendships, he will identify more and more with the radical ideology that is taught in the group by its charismatic leader. Old living habits, contacts, and even ties to one's own family are possibly relinquished; the clothing style is Islamized; and all of life is checked for its conformity with the lifestyle of early Islamic society.

---

[44]   Marc Sageman. *Leaderless Jihad. Terror Networks in the twenty-first Century.* University of Pennsylvania Press: Philadelphia, 2008, p. 65.

3. The indoctrination phase

During the phase of indoctrination, the radical opinions of the jihadist group are completely accepted. The use of violence against the west, against "the infidels," is something that at this stage is openly discussed and seen by all members as a necessarily acceptable means of defense. *Jihad* is declared to be an individual responsibility that every Muslim is to fight. This is in order to erect the true faith and a life according to the commands of the *sharia.* Changes in concrete life circumstances are announced to the newly indoctrinated jihadists by the leaders, and the soon approaching dawn of a time of well-being is promised to come by means of a necessary action.

Usually the members of the group no longer meet in a mosque during the indoctrination phase. Rather, they meet somewhere else, e.g., in a private residence. This is the case since other Muslims, in light of the group's own radical judgment, are now seen to have moved into the vicinity of the infidels. The internet provides additional information about the opportunities for conducting some sort of attack, and there are videos of martyrs who have successfully undertaken attacks. In this way the internet serves as an accelerator to radicalization; its messages, however, address people who are already radicalized members of a conspiratorial group.

4. Taking action

By the time the fourth phase begins, individual members have accepted their participation in *jihad*. For them *jihad* is no longer a war of aggression but rather one of defense, even if there are civilians who die in the course of action. The goal is to set up a "just" society, which stands in direct opposition to the present society. The world "out there," with its demonic powers, is rejected, and a feeling arises that one's own group is living under an acute threat. The utopian world order of tomorrow appears to move into reachable proximity, and the small avant-garde is in the position to bring about this better future via a battle against the powers of evil.[45]

The final phase up to the time of planning and conducting an attack can take a very short amount of time. Videos about *jihad*, blogs, and forums can also play an important role in this phase. The attack is planned in concrete terms, and the roles the different members of the group will play are defined. Frequently a will is composed, or a farewell video is made. Once

---

[45] According to Rudolph Peters who summarizes the situation in the Netherlands. "Dutch Extremist Islamism: Van Gogh's Murderer and His ideas" in Rik Coolsaet. *Jihadi Terrorism and the Radicalisation Challenge in Europe.* Ashgate: Aldershot, 2008, pp. 109-114, here c. 126.

all of this has happened, the "point of no return" has been reached. Group dynamics play a significant role, such that at this point no person leaves the group. Whether an attack is carried out appears to lie most essentially with the determination of the spiritual mentor.

The process of radicalization can occur quietly and unnoticed. There are no clear signs. Withdrawal from society, an Islamic style of dress, an intensive imitation of Mohammed's life, and the breaking of contact with the family could be serious warning signs. However, they are by themselves not clear indicators of entry into a jihadist group.

Radical groups offer clear rules and simple images of the enemy, an elite identity, commitment to an alleged just cause, a place in society in this world, admiration by the Muslim community, and the reestablishment of the "natural" order in which "true" Islam and the order of the *sharia* will achieve the victory. The radicalized group becomes a "picture of the afterlife" and a better world for believers, with the goal of producing a "pure" Islamic society according to Mohammed's model. It offers a home, true friendship, and a new family to the uprooted individual. This is its greatest attraction.

D. Integration as a counteracting force against Islamism and jihadism

Jihadism is a real threat to the peace and security of Europe and much of the world. The battle against this threat is not going to be won simply by hunting down terrorists, by devising better security systems, and by implementing effective systems to monitor suspects, although these are, of course, important measures for protecting the general public. The battle against terror will only be won by drying out the fertile soil in which it grows. This fertile soil is the jihadist teaching that falls upon a part of the immigrant community.

Over against the western world, the feeling among immigrants is one of permanent estrangement, and in cultures shaped by Islam, there is a great amount of bottled-up anger. The officially disclosed double standards pursued by Superpower and occupying forces in Iraq (keywords here are Guantanamo Bay, Abu Ghraib, rejection of the arbitration awards by the International Court of Justice) at the same time that a "crusade" against the "axis of evil" is pursued are together interpreted to comprise a campaign to destroy Islam. The consequence is not only a feeling of humiliation, but also hostility toward, as well as internal emigration from, the European host societies.

Germany is still suffering the long-term consequences of its decades-long, politically fostered, and readily publicly believed illusion that *Gas-*

tarbeiter (guest workers) only have temporary residence. In addition, there are the long-term consequences of not having undertaken steps early enough to promote integration and to improve the language ability of *Gastarbeiter* in an effort to offer those uprooted a permanent home. A consequence of denying the awareness of permanent life together was an indifference toward political networks which made use of this vacuum in order to commit immigrants to their agenda. This meant, among other things, seclusion from western society. This agenda meets with such sympathy among immigrants, because their talk of being sealed off from and of withdrawing from western society, as well as their condemnation of western society, makes it all too easy to align with the everyday experience of many immigrants.[46] Ed Husain has stated how this was the case for Great Britain in the 1980s: "*Having been sealed off from Great Britain and isolated from the eastern culture of our parents, Islamism gave us a place and a meaning in life.*"[47] This meaning and sense of place in life is something that is experienced far too rarely in western societies. A jihadist group provides a counterweight in this respect:

> "In the place of being aimlessly driven and of searching for egocentric pleasures, their members become part of a collective and challenging project, which mobilizes all their enthusiasm, their commitment, and their readiness to sacrifice. That is what civil society does not find easy to offer: a place within a community which offers acceptance and a sense of belonging and affords their lives purpose and meaning."[48]

If a radical group offers the feeling of community and if it functions in a way that offers meaning in an environment that, on the basis of personal and economic crises, is otherwise experienced as senseless and empty, the step to radicalization in a group of like-minded people can be a very short one: "*Young people with a great need for belonging and acceptance are exposed to a 'bombardment of love' ... love, acceptance and personal confirmation and integration in a brotherhood or sisterhood of friends.*"[49] Owing to this hotbed, the potential for radicalization among Muslims in Germany and other countries is not negligible, even if at present only about 1% of Muslims are members of an extremist group. However, given the

---

[46] So also Quintan Wiktorowicz: *Al-Muhajiroun and Radical Islam*, p. 5 (http://insct. syr.edu/Projects/islam-ihl/research/Wiktorowicz.Joining%20the%20Cause.pdf) (accessed December 21, 2009).

[47] Husain. *Islamist*. op. cit., p. 73.

[48] Karsten Hundeide. "Becoming a committed Insider" in Culture & Psychology 9/2003, pp. 107-129, here p. 123.

[49] Ibid., p. 113.

diverse factors that can lead to radicalization, the latent potential for a po-
litico-religiously motivated radicalization in Germany, according to the
study "Muslims in Germany," cannot be easily quantified. Nevertheless,
the authors, by virtue of the comprehensive nature of data collection during
the years 2004-2007, assume this group could amount to approximately
10% -12% of the Muslims in Germany, which would mean between
350,000 and 500,000 people.[50]

In the area of politics, on the one hand, there have to be negotiations in
order to place sensible limits on the building of oversized mosques. Inflat-
ed demands made on the state have to be staved off after what has already
been an expansion of minority rights, and clear integration expectations
need to be held out to counter the victim mentality of a number of Muslim
groups. Laws and their consistent application, monitoring, and the prohibition of radical groups are indispensable components for the security of
Europe. But these measures alone are not sufficient to win the "battle for
the minds and hearts of the Muslim community"[51] and to dry up the not
insignificant radicalization potential so that in the future fewer people turn
away from a society where they sense they are discriminated against as
marginal figures.

The challenge that lies before us is that of allowing Islamic immigrants
to "arrive" in the middle, not on the margins, of our society. For this to
occur, some preconditions must be fulfilled, such as increased education
and a readiness to be decidedly and permanently engaged in society. The
more role models that can be produced, the more permeable the barriers
become, and the more attractive society can be made, the more impeded
radical groups will become and the more people will be able to resist the
lethal message of destruction and *jihad*. That is the common challenge for
every single one of us and for western society as a whole.

---

[50]   Brettfeld; Wetzels. *Muslime*. op. cit., p. 494.
[51]   Sageman. *Jihad*. op. cit., p. 94.

Literature on the topic of Islamism or political Islam

Holger Albrecht; Kevin Köhler (eds.) *Politischer Islam im Vorderen Orient. Zwischen Sozialbewegung, Opposition und Widerstand. Weltreligionen im Wandel 5.* Nomos: Baden-Baden, 2008

Katrin Brettfeld; Peter Wetzels. *Muslime in Deutschland. Eine Studie des Bundesinnenministeriums zu Integration, Integrationsbarrieren, Religion und Einstellungen zu Demokratie, Rechtsstaat und politisch-religiös motivierter Gewalt.* Hamburg: 2007.

Rik Coolsaet. *Jihadi Terrorism and the Radicalisation Challenge in Europe.* Ashgate: Aldershot, 2008.

Julia Gerlach. *Zwischen Pop und Dschihad. Muslimische Jugendliche in Deutschland.* Lizenzausgabe Bundeszentrale für politische Bildung: Bonn, 2006.

Islamismus. Texte zur Inneren Sicherheit. Bundesministerium des Innern. Berlin, 2004/2.

Volker Foertsch; Klaus Lange (eds.) *Islamistischer Terrorismus. Bestandsaufnahme und Bekämpfungsmöglichkeiten. Berichte und Studien der Hanns Seidel Stiftung, 86.* Akademie für Politik und Zeitgeschehen: München, 2005.

Ed Husain. *The Islamist. Why I joined radical Islam in Britain, what I saw inside and why I left.* Penguin Books: London, 2007.

Hamed Abdel-Samad. *Mein Abschied vom Himmel. Aus dem Leben eines Muslims in Deutschland.* Köln: Fackelträger, 2009.

Johannes Grundmann. *Islamische Internationalisten. Strukturen und Aktivitäten der Muslimbruderschaft und der islamischen Weltliga.* Reichert: Wiesbaden, 2005.

Gudrun Krämer: *Gottes Staat als Republik. Reflexionen zeitgenössischer Muslime zu Islam, Menschenrechten und Demokratie.* Nomos: Baden-Baden, 1999.

Ivesa Lübben. „Die ägyptische Muslimbruderschaft – Auf dem Weg zur politischen Partei" in Holger Albrecht; Kevin Köhler (eds.) *Politischer Islam im Vorderen Orient. Zwischen Sozialbewegung, Opposition und Widerstand. Weltreligionen im Wandel 5.* Nomos: Baden-Baden, 2008, pp. 75-97.

Reinhard Möller (ed.) *Islamismus und Terroristische Gewalt.* Bibliotheca Academica, Reihe Orientalistik, Band 8. Ergon: Würzburg, 2004.

Muslimisches Leben in Deutschland, published by the Bundesamt für Migration und Flüchtlinge (Federal Office for Migration and Refugees). Nürnberg: 2009.

Oliver Roy; Antoine Sfeir (eds.) *The Columbia World Dictionary of Islamism.* Columbia University Press: New York, 2007.

Marc Sageman. *Leaderless Jihad. Terror Networks in the twenty-first Century.* University of Pennsylvania Press: Philadelphia, 2008.

Guido Steinberg. *Islamismus und islamistischer Terrorismus im Nahen und Mittleren Osten. Ursachen der Anschläge vom 11. September 2001.* Konrad-Adenauer-Stiftung, Zukunftsforum Politik Nr. 39, St. Augustin: 2002.

Guido Steinberg. *Der nahe und der ferne Feind. Die Netzwerke des islamistischen Terrorismus.* C. H. Beck: München, 2005.

Thomas Tartsch. *Islamischer Fundamentalismus und Jihadismus – Bedrohung der Inneren Sicherheit? Reihe Politik, Band 2.* Europäischer Universitätsverlag: Bochum, 2005.

W. Montgomery Watt. *Islamic Fundamentalism and Modernity.* Routledge: London, 1989.

Wendelin Wenzel-Teuber. *Islamische Ethik und moderne Gesellschaft im Islamismus von Yusuf al-Qaradawi. Nur al-hikma, Interdisziplinäre Schriftenreihe zur Islamwissenschaft, Bd. 2.* Verlag Dr. Kovac: Hamburg, 2005.

Hans Zehetmair (ed.) *Der Islam im Spannungsfeld von Konflikt und Dialog.* Verlag für Sozialwissenschaften: Wiesbaden, 2005.

Biography

Prof. **Christine Schirrmacher, PhD** is an international scholar of Islamic Studies, currently teaching as Professor of Islamic Studies at the Institute of Asian and Oriental Studies, Department of Islamic Studies and Near Eastern Languages of the State University of Bonn, Germany and the Evangelical-Theological Faculty (ETF) (Protestant University) at Leuven, Belgium. In 2013 she was teaching as Professor of Islamic Studies at the University of Erfurt, Germany, and in 2014, as a Guest Professor at the University of Tuebingen, Germany.

She studied Islamic Studies, comparative religions, history and modern literature and holds an M. A. and a PhD in Islamic Studies. Her doctoral dissertation dealt with the Muslim-Christian controversy in the 19th and 20th century, her thesis for her postdoctoral lecture qualification ("Habilitation") focused on contemporary Muslim theological voices on apostasy, human rights and religious freedom.

She regularly lectures on Islam and security issues at different government institutions of security policy in Germany. Recently, she has been appointed to the "Academic Advisory Council of the Federal Agency for Civic Education" by the German Federal Minister of the Interior. She also teaches at the Academy of Foreign Affairs of the Foreign Office in Berlin, Germany and is a consultant to different advisory bodies of society and politics, e.g. to the Human Rights Committee of the "Bundestag", Berlin, Germany, i. e. the German Federal Parliament.

She is director of the International Institute of Islamic Studies (IIIS) of the World Evangelical Alliance (WEA) and its regional counterpart, the "Institut für Islamfragen" (Institute of Islamic Affairs) of the German, Swiss and Austrian Evangelical Alliance, as well as "Commissioner for Islamic Affairs" for WEA.

She has visited many Muslim majority countries, has been guest lecturer at a number of universities worldwide and speaker at national as well as international conferences dealing with Islam, held by non-religious, Christian and Muslim organisations.

She has widely published on the subjects of Islamic theology as well as comparisons between Islamic and Christian theology, on political Islam and Islamism, on Islam and democracy, on women in Islamic societies, on sharia law, on human rights in Islam and on integration and radicalization of Muslims in Europe. Besides many scholarly articles, she published about 15 books in German, translated into English, Spanish, Kiswahili, Romanian and Korean.

Her two volume introduction "Der Islam – Geschichte, Lehre, Unterschiede zum Christentum" (1994/2003) (*Islam – History, Dogmatics, Differences to Christianity*) is widely used at seminaries and in educational programs. Among her recent publications are "Frauen und die Scharia – Die Menschenrechte im Islam" (2004/2006) (*Women and Sharia Law – Human Rights in Islam*), "Der Islam – eine Einführung" (2005) (*Islam – A Short Introduction*), "Die Scharia – Recht und Gesetz im Islam" (2008) (*The Sharia – Law and Order in Islam*), "Islamismus – Wenn Glaube zur Politik wird" (2010) (*Islamism – When Faith turns out to be Politics*), and "Islam und Demokratie – ein Gegensatz?" (2013) (*Islam and Democracy – an Antagonism?*).